**NEW DIRECTIONS
FOR PROGRAM
EVALUATION**

Number 9 • 1981

NEW DIRECTIONS FOR PROGRAM EVALUATION

A Quarterly Sourcebook
Scarvia B. Anderson, Editor-in-Chief

Number 9, 1981

Assessing and Interpreting Outcomes

Samuel Ball
Guest Editor

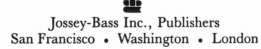
Jossey-Bass Inc., Publishers
San Francisco • Washington • London

ASSESSING AND INTERPRETING OUTCOMES
New Directions for Program Evaluation
Number 9, 1981
　　　Samuel Ball, Guest Editor

New Directions for Program Evaluation (publication number
USPS 449-050) is published quarterly by Jossey-Bass Inc., Publishers.
Subscriptions are available at the regular rate for institutions,
libraries, and agencies of $30 for one year. Individuals may
subscribe at the special professional rate of $18 for one year.

Correspondence:
Subscriptions, single-issue orders, change of address notices,
undelivered copies, and other correspondence should be sent to
New Directions Subscriptions, Jossey-Bass Inc., Publishers,
433 California Street, San Francisco, California 94104.

Editorial correspondence should be sent to the Editor-in-Chief,
Scarvia B. Anderson, Educational Testing Service, 250 Piedmont
Avenue, Suite 2020, Atlanta, Georgia 30308.

Library of Congress Catalogue Card Number LC 80-84296
International Standard Serial Number ISSN 0164-7989
International Standard Book Number ISBN 87589-856-4

Cover design by Willi Baum
Manufactured in the United States of America

Contents

Editor's Notes

"The proof of the pudding is in the eating." This is an excellent example of Grandma's and Grandpa's evaluation theory. Grandma and Grandpa are evaluators of considerable skill, cunning, and experience. They know a great deal about evaluating the outcomes of programs, culinary and otherwise. However, as we shall see, they evaluate in the older, informal style. They do not subscribe to our modish evaluation models.

Perhaps it is churlish to raise doubts about our lovable and elderly grandparents' evaluation skills, but grandparent evaluation theory does have its problems. For one thing, it is too general to enable us to make specific predictions, as we shall see when we examine their contention that the proof of the pudding (read "program") is in the eating (read "intended outcomes").

Let me illustrate a few of the major problems by telling you a true story about a family get-together we had at my grandparents' place last Christmas. First there was the exchange of gifts. After the exclamations of delight ("How did you know I needed that?" "Wow! What great colors!"), I put away the five pairs of red socks I'd been given and we settled down to a dinner that promised to be good.

In true ecumenical style, we began with chicken soup that savored a little of minestrone. Then we had a large turkey with Yorkshire pudding smothered with champignons. But the *pièce de résistance* was the great plum pudding my grandparents had lovingly made. It was a very rich plum pudding, very English actually, with a marvelous creamy custard to embellish it. I thought it was lovely and began eating with relish. My sister, unfortunately, is one of those patronizingly superior beings who think with dogmatic devotion that bony is beautiful. (I happen to be slightly overweight.) Though it almost broke Grandma's heart and disturbed Grandpa's sense of loyalty, my sister insisted on merely picking at the plum pudding, claiming with the chirpy persistence of a caged canary that dinner was already too calorific. "A small piece of fruit would be an excellent dessert," she added gratuitously. I determined that next year I would smuggle into the dinner party, just for her, a grape.

My cousin got married last year to a rather sickly fellow who wheezes and rattles. "I'm allergic to dried fruit, but I'll try the custard," he said. "It looks good, that plum pudding, but I can't have any. It'd make me break out and I'd choke." "Try it anyway," I suggested pleasantly. My cousin gave me a nasty look.

Uncle Giuseppi isn't part of my family, really. He's from Naples originally, and he put down our concrete paths years ago. He was so hardworking and alone that we rather adopted him. He looked at the plum pudding the way he would look at newfangled, premixed concrete. "Do you have some vino or Galliano I can pour over the pudding?" he asked. Grandma said no, and Giuseppi said he'd just have some coffee.

My niece (my sister's daughter) is the kind of girl who takes up very little space. Turn her sideways and she disappears. "I want some plum pudding, Gramps," she said, to everyone's surprise. "But not now. I couldn't eat another thing. Could you wrap it up for me and I'll have it tomorrow for lunch?" We weren't surprised anymore.

Suddenly my father, who was steadily eating his plum pudding, burped. My mother shuddered and looked threateningly at him. "Sign of satisfaction, m'dear," he said. "It's meant as a compliment to the cook."

"It's boorish and disgusting," said Mother, with an attempt to achieve finality in the conversation. But Father, getting his second wind, burped again. He smiled at everyone amiably, even my mother. "Truly the best plum pudding I've tasted all year. A three-star plum pudding, I'd rate it. No, not three star. Three burp." And, to my mother's consternation, he made good his rating.

Meanwhile, I finished my portion of plum pudding. I said that I had evaluated it as excellent on the basis of my tastebuds (not my burps). Grandpa said he agreed wholeheartedly that it was excellent. Grandma, however, never touched hers. It is her tradition. "I get my pleasure out of making it," she assured us again. "After making it, I just don't feel like eating it. But I do like to see you enjoy eating it." She'll say the same thing next year.

Later that evening, with the dishes all put away, we sat around the fire and talked about the nice day we'd had together. "And what did you think of my pudding?" asked Grandma.

My professional responsibilities include evaluating programs, not pudding, but I nonetheless listened to the ensuing family discussion with interest. There were many lessons to be learned.

"The proof of the pudding is in the eating," said Grandpa with great aplomb. "I did the dishes, and I can say that the high quality of that pudding was made clear by the way this mob, with one or two exceptions [a baleful look at my sister], polished off the pudding."

"Nonsense," said my sister. "Everyone is too polite. Just because they consumed that calorific compound doesn't mean they enjoyed it — or that it was good for them. And even if they enjoyed it — even if we evaluate the pudding in terms of the eater's satisfaction — we'd be making a gross mistake. The proof of the pudding cannot be estimated properly by using such short-run measures as those embodied in the eating. We must look at what it does for us in the long run. And I say that the plum pudding will make us fat and unhealthy. The proof of the pudding cannot be estimated by interviewing eaters or by such nonreactive measures as the state of the pudding plates when they are about to be taken from the table to the dishwasher."

"Fruit (and nuts) to you, Sister," I said, trying to be both unpleasant and witty. "I don't agree with you and your elitist views. What do you say, Grandma?"

Grandma looked at me gratefully. "I'm glad you asked, Sonny," she said. "I think that short-run measures like the eating and the amount left on the plate are nonsense. Likewise, however, I think that long-term measures like increase in subcutaneous fat tissues are nonsense, too." (Granny likes using big words to show she's not senile.) "What I think is that the outcome is not really that important — not to me, anyway. I find that the truly important matter to consider in evaluating plum pudding is not the outcome per se but the process. I love making the pudding. It gives me a feeling of involvement, of being part of the future, of being useful. It gives me something nice to do. Who cares if you give it a 6 out of 10 or a 7 out of 10? Not me."

Uncle Giuseppi took up the challenge of measuring the value of the plum pudding with true European style. "Ah, Granny," he said, "I'm so glad you enjoy making the pudding. And I'd never disagree with you about mixing the pudding. I mean, we have so much in common. I got so much fun over the years mixing the concrete." Grandfather, with empathy for Grandmother, winced. Uncle Giuseppi, however, just winked at us all. Then he said, "As for this argument about the outcome measure — short- or long-term, that's not the most important thing to consider. What is important is where you come from. Now, I come from Italy, and we don't like plum pudding. If I came from England, I would like it. Same plum pudding, but different evaluations. If you want a good evaluation of your plum pudding, get in an English eater. If you don't, get in an Italian one. That's my message. It's not the outcome. It's where the evaluator comes from that counts."

My cousin's allergic husband got into the act now. "Uncle Giuseppi's partly right," he said patronizingly. "But it isn't just where the eater comes from but what he carries with him. I mean, I grew up in London, so, according to Uncle Giuseppi, I should have liked the plum pudding. But I have this allergy, see. So if it were just based on where you come from, you'd be making a mistake predicting my evaluation."

My niece thought about this a bit and said, "I think you're all wrong. I judge the pudding not by the eating and not on the basis of where I come from or who I am. I judge it entirely on the basis of how it looks from an objective viewpoint. I mean, I don't like eating that much anyway. But I do like looking at the food. That plum pudding looked magnificent, Granny. Especially the way the custard caressed it as it ran down the side. I mean, who cares what these crumbs thought of it as they ate it? I could tell by looking it was a great pudding."

My father had listened to this family conversation with apparent lack of interest. It was startling when he looked at Mother and said, "I'd like to air my opinion now." And for the fourth time that afternoon, he burped.

Mother was about to unravel, as we all could see, so we were glad that Grandfather took a hand. "Enough!" he said. "I want no more of this stupid argument about how to evaluate a plum pudding. We've heard from me, Sister, Grandma, Uncle Giuseppi, Cousin's husband, Niece, and Father. You can argue all you like about how to measure outcomes. It's a stupid argument. You have all got to realize that, in measuring outcomes, it is all relative!"

It seems to me there is a lot to learn about outcomes in program evaluation from my family reunion last Christmas. The subsequent chapters will provide academic and scholarly detail to formalize the folksy approach taken, I hope inoffensively, in this introduction. The reader will note, I hope, a few principles concerning outcomes in program evaluation. Let me, at the risk of being too much like a teacher, suggest a few of the principles that my family party and the succeeding chapters present. Let me request this listing be seen as partial and that you, the reader, expand it.

1. Outcomes that are directly related to program purposes satisfy mainly those directly involved in deciding the purposes.
2. Outcomes that are unintended by program developers can be of vital interest, at least to some observers or decision makers.
3. For some, program outcomes are less impressive than the program's processes in evaluating the program's worth.
4. For others, it is what the program looks like, *in situ,* that is most important—not what it actually does for its clients.

5. Program outcomes are in part defined by the academic discipline and professional training of the evaluator.
6. Program outcomes are in part defined by the personal values and interests of the evaluator.
7. There is unlikely to be complete agreement, even with simple programs, about what constitutes their proper outcome measures.

The issues of who defines the program outcomes of interest — and the predilections they bring to the process — will be discussed further and exemplified in the chapters that follow. In the first chapter, Cline and Sinnott, a sociologist and a psychologist, explore the special problems of identifying complex outcomes in complex organizations and the methodologies that can be employed to determine whether such outcomes have been realized. They focus particularly on the assessment of organizational change and draw on their experiences in examining the impact of automation on the structure and functioning of academic libraries.

In the next chapter, Levine, an economist, argues that many important program decisions cannot be based on measures of outcome alone, but require systematic comparison of the cost of producing outcomes to the value these outcomes yield over time. In the course of the discussion, he provides evaluators who may be unsophisticated in economics with a useful vocabulary and an understanding of the concepts involved.

Sechrest and Yeaton come to their task from backgrounds in psychology and experiences in evaluating a wide variety of health and other human services programs. They counsel us on the necessity of considering the size of outcomes — immediate and long-range, and over different parts of the scale. And they describe several approaches to estimating whether effects are large enough to be of any social importance.

In the fourth chapter, Kiresuk, Lund, and Schultz, all from the Program Evaluation Research Center, which is concerned largely with health programs, emphasize the role of the consumer in formulation and evaluation of program outcomes.

Finally, in the last chapter, I review some guiding principles derived from my own experiences in assessing educational outcomes and add some further thoughts on the size of outcome effects. Evaluators are frequently too ambitious about the number of outcome variables they can handle effectively and are almost always confronted with unrealistic expectations about the effects a program can produce.

I believe that the diversity of backgrounds and views reflected in the chapters in this sourcebook will extend and enhance evaluators' appreciation of both the possibilities and the pitfalls they will face in their efforts to document the "proof of the program."

Samuel Ball
Guest Editor

Samuel Ball is professor and head, Department of Education, at the University of Sydney, Australia. He is also editor of the Journal of Educational Psychology. *He has coauthored books and articles on program evaluation with the series editor, Scarvia Anderson.*

*Methods useful in identifying and assessing outcomes
of relatively simple programs may not be practical
or appropriate for complex programs and systems.
Comparative case study methods are recommended
for dealing with such global outcomes
of planned organizational change.*

What Can We Learn About Change in Organizations?

Hugh F. Cline
Loraine T. Sinnott

Most evaluation research projects attempt to assess the impact of some type of intervention or treatment program upon individuals. The focus of the research described here is to assess the impact of planned social change upon collectivities of individuals.

Conceptually, this focus is identical to that employed in a research project that assesses the impact of a children's television program on reading readiness of preschool children, the negative income-tax experiment on the work behavior of recipients, or a comprehensive medical insurance program upon the physical and mental health of the participants. When one attempts to do evaluation research on complex organizations, a number of methodological and practical problems emerge in the identification of important outcomes.

This chapter discusses these problems by drawing upon the authors' recent experience in research examining the impact of automation on the structure and functioning of academic libraries. We begin the discussion with a brief review of alternative research strategies. The design we have found most useful in our research activities is that of comparative case studies. This approach is described in detail in the remaining sections of the chapter.

There are four basic research methodologies that can be used to examine change in complex organizations—quasiexperiments, surveys, simulations, and case studies. In a field setting, quasiexperiments approximate the characteristics of a true experiment, including (1) application of treatments or stimuli to an experimental group with attendant control groups that do not receive the stimulus; (2) random assignment of a large number of subjects or units of analysis to the experimental and control groups; and (3) collection of measurements, usually pre- and postexperiment, to determine differences in outcomes.

The quasiexperiment has been used in many evaluation research projects. Data analyses in quasiexperiments usually entail some type of multivariate statistical techniques, and the assumptions underlying such analyses require a substantial number of cases, usually at least thirty. It is frequently practical to use this design in field settings with large numbers of individual subjects. However, when organizations are the units of analysis, it is seldom feasible to accomplish random assignment to experimental and control groups. The problems involved in getting thirty or more organizations to agree to participate in a randomized experiment are next to insurmountable.

A second possible methodology for evaluation in organizational settings is the questionnaire survey. Although this method has been used with some success, it is extremely difficult to use effectively unless the investigator is thoroughly familiar with the organization. It is usually difficult to determine both the relevant questions to ask members of organizations and the appropriate vocabulary. In order to design questionnaire items, one must be aware of the structure and functioning of an organization, as well as its unique practices and local jargon. A great deal of information is usually required from each organization, and completion of a questionnaire will typically demand a substantial commitment of institutional resources. Unless some substantive or financial incentive is given to the organizations, it is most unlikely that they will comply.

A third methodology available for organizational evaluation is simulation. Models or theories about organizations are postulated, and a conclusion or set of conclusions is logically derived. Frequently the conclusion results from "running the model" or simulating certain aspects of the organization's functioning on a computer. The experience of social and behavioral scientists with simulations is still too limited to assess the eventual contribution of this relatively new methodology, but many scholars are optimistic about its potential. However, simulations cannot yet be used for assessing the impact of planned social change upon organizations. In organizational evaluations, the investigator is usually interested in observing a wide variety of anticipated and unanticipated consequences of change, and it is precisely in the area of unanticipated outcomes that simulations are weakest. Any model represents only selected aspects of the phenomena under study and therefore is limited in the outcomes that can be observed.

The fourth design available is the case study. The intensive study of selected examples characterizes the case study. It is particularly fruitful for stimulating insights, suggesting hypotheses for future research, and identifying major consequences of planned social change. The power of the case study is dramatically enhanced when it includes several sites for comparison. In the comparative design, the investigator examines in detail a small number of organizations using a comparable set of data collection techniques, including interviews, observations, and analysis of existing reports and statistical data.

For the reasons given, experimental, survey, and simulation designs are often not practical for studying most types of planned organizational change. The case study methodology is a feasible alternative. This chapter discusses the comparative case study approach, highlighting its strengths and weaknesses, describing procedures and approaches, and suggesting where the methodology needs to be further refined.

The case study is a frequently used and much maligned method in the social sciences. Clinicians have produced many rich case studies of individuals; sociologists and political scientists use the method effectively in studies of organizations; and the anthropological literature is replete with countless ethnographies of societies. But there are a number of major problems inherent in the case study method, the most important being its limited generalizability. Because a case study is an in-depth investigation that requires a substantial commitment of time and resources, it is usually very expensive. Comparative case studies are even more expensive. Thus, they are usually confined to a small number of units of analysis; in our case, a small number of organizations. Hence, whether it be a case study of one or of several organizations, the generalizability to other organizations is always questionable.

Investigators who employ organizational case study designs are also confronted with a number of other problems. It is frequently very difficult to get organizations to agree to participate in studies that necessarily interfere with day-to-day activities and could potentially produce embarrassing results. To participate in the investigation, an organization must commit resources, the major commitment usually being staff time. If some benefit would result from participation, resource allocation to the effort might be considered more favorably. A great deal of careful planning and diplomacy is required to obtain the cooperation of organizations in social science research, and the project should ensure that the organizations receive as payment something they value in addition to the dubious satisfaction of contributing to scientific progress. The researcher should consider what might be offered to an organization to encourage participation. A management report, private consultation, or even a transfer of money are all possible payments.

Since case studies examine organizations at one particular time, investigators must always confront the problem of collecting accurate historical data. The difficulties involved in eliminating biases in retrospective recall of past events are well known and documented (Jahoda and others, 1959). Meticulous planning of topics for inclusion in the interviews, careful delineation of objectives for observations, and skillful use of existing documents and reports are effective means for collecting data from multiple sources in order to verify the accuracy of historical information.

The problems of dealing with retrospective data are particularly troublesome, but they are examples of a more general class of problems concerning both the nature of the data collected and the analytical techniques employed in case studies. The remainder of this chapter is devoted to discussing these data collection and analysis problems to ensure that substantively important outcomes are not overlooked in studies assessing the impact of planned change in organizations.

At the most general level, we suggest a strategy that maximizes the comparability of comprehensive, objective data collection and analysis in each organization. It requires very careful advance planning of all interviews and observations and effective yet flexible adherence to data collection schedules. Data reduction and analysis must follow prespecified rules for verifying the accuracy of all information. Yet careful compliance to this general strategy and the many specific guidelines we derive and discuss still leave the investigator facing the very difficult question of precisely what information to collect in the case studies. By its very name, the case study implies comprehensive data collection. But this is impossible, for, in a very real sense, the amount of data that can be collected on an organization is infinite. Every investigator must select certain aspects of the organization to emphasize. In doing so, he or she implicitly decides all other aspects are either of secondary importance or will be ignored. In our view, these decisions should be made explicitly in advance of any data collecting and most emphatically included in the subsequent documentation of the project.

Drawing upon the work of Nielen, we have found it convenient to describe organizations using the following five interdependent dimensions: task, function, information, fiscal, and personnel (Nielen, 1977, pp. 169–175). Nielen briefly defined six dimensions of large-scale organizations relevant to curriculum design for information scientists. We have modified and extended his scheme for our purposes of studying organizations.

The task dimension describes an organization as a set of specific work assignments interconnected via authority and accountability relationships. To learn how an organization attempts to accomplish its goals, the investigator must identify the major tasks assigned to different units, locate the supervisor-supervisee relationships surrounding these tasks, and determine what specific activities are undertaken to accomplish the separate tasks. Data describing the task dimension are gathered both in interviews asking people what they do in their jobs and in observations of work activities. Equally important for describing the task dimension are the data collected from existing documents, such as job descriptions.

The function dimension describes an organization as interconnected multiple operating units and the organization's environment via stimulus-response relationships. To study the function dimension, the investigator must determine how the various units both within and outside the organization interact and the specific content of the stimuli and responses that characterize these relationships. Interviews, observations, and documentary evidence such as organization charts and annual reports can all be used to describe the function dimension. In contrast with the task dimension, which focuses on activities in particular units of the organization, the function dimension describes how these units interrelate and, in concert, achieve the organization's goals.

The information dimension portrays an organization as a structure of decision points connected via data channels. Organizations must carefully distribute decision-making points among their members and then design, implement, and monitor data channels to ensure that decision makers have access to all relevant information. To examine this dimension, the investigator must locate the decision makers, map both the formal and informal data channels, and tactfully "bug" a sample of the communication lines. The responsible and objective study of the information dimension is undoubtedly the most sensitive and difficult aspect of organizational case studies.

The fiscal dimension depicts the organization as monetary resources connected via budgetary and accounting relations. To study the fiscal dimension, the investigator must determine how resources are allocated in the organization. The details of budget deliberations and decisions are most illuminating of the process of resource allocation. Existing documents may describe some of these procedures, but interviews with both those who prepare budgets and those who approve them are crucial. In addition, the investigator must be alert to the possibility of "hidden resource allocation." A substantial portion of an organization's resources are often allocated in a way that is not readily apparent in studying an institution's budget. Budgets usually emphasize revenues and expenditures and do not always depict overall resource allocation. It is important to review all financial statements, including capital expenditures, longer-range fiscal projections, and statements of changes and balances in various funds.

The last dimension, the personnel dimension, characterizes an organization as a group of persons connected via behavior relations. The most important means of collecting data on this dimension is observation of interpersonal interactions. However, observing the full panoply of interpersonal interactions in even a very small organization would require an inordinate amount of time. Therefore, the investigator must prudently select the most important interactions and choose appropriate time periods for observations.

These five dimensions are not exhaustive of all aspects of an organization's structure and functioning that may be relevant to examining the impact of planned social change. They are highly interdependent and therefore not mutually exclusive. Nevertheless, they provide an investigator with a series of options for data collection and analysis in organizational case studies, and they cover the major characteristics of the structure and functioning of all organizations.

The remainder of this chapter consists of our counsel as to relevant considerations and optimal strategies for conducting comparative organizational case studies. Our advice is based upon recent studies of the impact of automation upon academic libraries. The next section discusses our experience in selecting organizations for inclusion, approaching them and gaining their participation, and collecting and organizing the data. Then we briefly explore the problems of reducing and analyzing the vast and rich arrays of information collected in case studies. Finally, we present a number of recommendations for further strengthening and refining the methodology of comparative organizational case studies.

Conducting Comparative Case Studies

The goal of the research we are describing is to identify structural and functional changes in organizations that result when a given program is implemented. Such changes could be inferred by selecting an organization that is about to introduce a program and observing it at a number of points during implementation. But this approach is not always an option. Resources may be too limited for such a design, or the information may be needed more rapidly than a longitudinal analysis allows. Often the support needed to begin an investigation is not available until after organizational changes are in progress, have halted, or have been fully assimilated.

Structural and functional changes may also be inferred through a comparative case study design. This approach also requires support for field activities, but site visits need occur only once, and spacing of visits over time is not necessary. In this section, we detail the methods of comparative case studies.

Selecting a Sample. In a comparative design, outcomes are inferred by examining institutions in various stages of program implementation. Limiting the sample to organizations comparable on the five dimensions mentioned prior to program introduction will simplify the task of identifying program outcomes. Furthermore, the investigation can minimize falsely attributing outcomes to the program by selecting sites not experiencing other transformations (such as a recent change in senior administration or physical plant). But the researcher will seldom have the luxury of either comparability or stability. Organizations develop independently, and variety should be anticipated. Many of their numerous idiosyncrasies will be appreciated only after fieldwork is well under way. The dynamic quality of organizations makes it extremely unlikely that they will be stable in all other respects except program implementation. The validity of outcomes identified as program outcomes will depend on the investigator's success at ferreting out the effects of noncomparability of sites and activities that compete to change structure and functioning.

Other factors acting to compromise an ideal configuration of sites include resource limitations and the reluctance of some sites to participate in the investigation. Often the number of organizations the investigator would like to examine exceeds the number the project budget can accommodate. The latter number can be calculated by first estimating the time needed to collect, synthesize, and analyze data for one institution. Divided into total project resources for data collection and analysis, this estimate sets an upper limit to sample size. If that limit jeopardizes the reliability and validity of findings, one might choose to narrow the project's scope, paring the data collection activities and thus decreasing the amount of time needed at any one institution.

Receptiveness to participate in the project will vary across the population of institutions. Evaluation findings may result in the reduction or termination of program funding; they may result in pressures to alter the way resources are allocated. Participation may provide a forum for displaying accomplishments. The increased visibility that accompanies participation can be viewed as a threat or an an opportunity, depending considerably on the types of problems the organization has experienced during program implementation, its willingness to modify organizational appendages that have grown as a result of the program, and the personalities of senior administrators.

Because participation is for some a risk while a benefit for others, relying on volunteers may result in a biased sample. Yet in most settings, no feasible alternative exists. To examine an organization requires the permission of its management. Reluctant administrators may be pressured by external forces to cooperate, but the ill feelings resulting from coercion could seriously interfere with the investigation. It is not difficult for management to impede the researcher's efforts.

An often-used procedure for identifying candidates for participation is to contact individuals known to have specialized knowledge regarding the organizations. These individuals can facilitate introductions to new contacts. In this snowball fashion, the researcher can compile a list of candidates. A risk in this technique is entering a network of organizations that does not adequately represent the entire population of organizations. One can reduce this risk by including among the contacts individuals known to have a global perspective. For example, if the organizations have a national association, officers of that association are likely to have the range of knowledge desired.

Approaching the Organizations. Letters of introduction that include project goals, proposed on-site research activities, and references, which may be employed to assess the researcher's credibility, are the optimal way to initiate contacts with organizations elected for the sample. Subsequent telephone calls may then be used to determine if the organization is interested in participating. Letters allow the organization's head thoughtfully to consider the invitation. They also provide a convenient vehicle for sharing the researcher's proposal with other senior administrators, should their advice be sought. A telephone call not preceded by a letter may force a decision without careful consideration of the implications of the response. The researcher may lose a participant that might have volunteered if given time to consider the proposal. But the project might gain a volunteer who, later realizing the impact of the commitment, terminates participation or, worse still, continues at a minimal level of cooperation. Another advantage of an introductory letter as opposed to a telephone call is that the researcher has more control over what is communicated in the message and how it is perceived. A telephone call is a dynamic event. Its content cannot be readily controlled or predicted. Furthermore, it may force the organization's head into an interaction at an inopportune time, increasing the likelihood of an unconsidered response.

Visits to potential participants prior to their decisions may result in fewer refusals. These visits allow administrators to meet the fieldwork team and discuss the project. The initial visit requries a lesser commitment of organization resources. Thus, there would be less reluctance to agree to such a meeting. Assuming the project staff successfully communicates its goals and mode of operation, the organization would probably be more reluctant to refuse participation later, since a precedent for committing resources to the project has already been established. The researcher can use the prefieldwork visits to learn more about the specific characteristics of the participant, information that may be crucial in planning subsequent fieldwork activities. During the visits, interviews might be conducted with senior staff members to gather these data. The collection of annual reports, statistical summaries, and other internally prepared documents will provide data complementing what is learned in the interviews.

Planning the Fieldwork. Planning the visits is greatly facilitated by detailed knowledge of organizational structure and functioning. It is difficult to identify appropriate informants for interviews and activities for observation without this information. If prefieldwork visits are not possible, plans for the fieldwork must rely upon information gleaned from organization charts, statistical summaries, annual reports, financial statements, and documents that provide functional descriptions of jobs or work units. Without such information, researchers may plan activities tangential to the project's overall goals or neglect important activities, thus significantly lowering project quality. Focusing in too narrowly may result in missing an unanticipated outcome. Furthermore, researchers naive to the full complexities of a situation may relinquish control of who is selected for interviewing and what is selected for observation to members of the organization who step forward to inform them of their ignorance, thus introducing biases and jeopardizing reliability.

To aid in accomplishing the fieldwork tasks, a schedule is necessary, although later adjustments may be required. The researcher will be entering a system in the midst of its operations. The organization cannot turn its attention solely to the evaluation efforts. Hence, the schedule will be subjected to the exigencies of the institution. Researchers will most certainly, in the course of the fieldwork, recognize or be directed to informants or activities that were not part of the original schedule. Although most activities of interest can be anticipated, some cannot, and the schedule should adapt to shifting priorities. The researcher who adheres strictly to a prearranged plan may miss opportunities to enrich the evaluation, but some discipline must be imposed to ensure all objectives are accomplished in the allotted time period.

To develop a schedule, it is helpful first to delineate the desired information and formulate the questions to be answered during fieldwork. Information and questions can then be associated with field procedures likely to satisfy them. Once procedures are enumerated, the schedule can be drawn.

Doing the Fieldwork. Fieldwork activities will typically include a combination of the following: interviews, observations of operations, observations of meetings, participation in organizational activities, and collection of documents produced by the organization. In most field research, interviews and observations account for the largest blocks of time.

Successful fieldwork depends upon interactions with individuals from various levels of the organizational hierarchy. They will vary in their degree of cooperation. A problem that must be anticipated is that staff will perceive the researcher as an arm of management, an evaluator who has come to assess their performance. This perception may provoke anxiety and self-consciousness among those who are being interviewed or observed and make some reluctant to give the requested information freely. If management is supportive of the research effort, this problem can be diminished by management's efforts to advise staff of project purposes. Fieldwork in organizations is thus both facilitated and encumbered by a commonly found structural feature—authority relationships. Such relationships provide a vehicle for messages to filter through the organization, passing from supervisor to supervisee, with their origin from above encouraging staff to attend to and abide by their content. But individuals may be reluctant to speak freely, fearing their confidences will be shared by supervisors.

The data collected from an individual during an interview depend on how the researcher is perceived. Indeed, the researcher's success will depend equally upon his or her procedures and ability to establish rapport. Because staff perception is so critical, the researcher may wish to do more than rely on the organization's administration to inform staff of the evaluation. Staff meetings in which the researcher discusses the project and answers questions provide an effective means for obtaining acceptance. This is a more efficient technique than talking to staff members individually. Furthermore, since individuals are exposed to the same information, more compatibility across interviews is ensured. Finally, group meetings held at the beginning of the fieldwork allow the research to be discussed in its early stages, thus preventing the spread of misinformation and rumors that may establish inaccurate ideas among staff members concerning project purposes.

The use of the data generated through interviews and observations and its confidentiality should be thoroughly explained to all individuals. These issues will be more salient for some than for others, but should be brought up with all, since it is difficult to predict the effects of such concerns on the responses and actions the researcher observes. Also, it is difficult to detect whether certain individuals harbor such concerns. The researcher may be reluctant to initiate discussion about these issues, anticipating that such a discussion will activate anxieties not present before or make individuals feel they are perceived as being exceptionally anxious. But inevitably the researcher will encounter persons who wish to know the researcher's responses to these questions and are inhibited from talking freely because of concerns about the use of their responses. If the researcher has an opportunity to hold staff meetings, the problems encountered in addressing confidentiality on an individual basis can be avoided by discussing these issues in a group setting.

The researcher may be concerned that observing individuals performing their jobs may result in self-consciousness. Some awkwardness will probably be experienced, but, as with *cinéma vérité*, the researchers' presence will soon be just another part of the worker's environment. Unobtrusiveness is essential if researchers wish to minimize the effect of their presence on the activities being observed.

Once the researcher begins to interview people in the organization, it will soon be evident that many people enjoy being interviewed by sympathetic and skilled interviewers. Many individuals like to discuss their roles in the organization, the activities in which they engage, and their attitudes concerning various aspects of the organization. Members of an organization seldom verbalize to an outsider their roles within and attitudes toward their workplace, and many appreciate the opportunity to do so. The novelty of discussing how one spends a considerable portion of one's life and what one's feelings are about the time spent will, for the most part, be considered not only enjoyable but also a personally rewarding experience. Of course, if the interviewees believe their responses may somehow be used against them, they will probably feel defensive and compliment the organization indiscriminately.

The researcher should undertake the interview with a schedule of topics, but the schedule should be treated much like the overall schedule of activities for the project; that is, it should be perceived as a guideline. Flexibly structured interviews are typically less anxiety-provoking than rigid situations, and the interview takes on characteristics of an informal conversation. Flexibly structured interviews also allow for unanticipated topics to surface. If the researcher believes the topics to be tangential, the conversation can be redirected. Because a researcher cannot anticipate all the relevant topics that should be addressed, the flexible interview format provides a vehicle to ensure that unanticipated outcomes of planned program changes are brought to the attention of the researcher.

In a flexibly structured interview, the researcher retains a set of topics for discussion and attempts to cover them. The "flow of conversation" can determine the order in which the topics are introduced. However, some structure within the interview is necessary to ensure that all topics are covered. Furthermore, since the reliability of interview data depends considerably on confirmation across interviews, structure is needed to provide a basis for comparison. In many ways, flexibly structured interviews demand more skill of the interviewer than more formal formats. The interviewer must conduct a casual conversation, smoothly directing a course through a set of predetermined topics and ensuring that this naturally evolving conversation generates all required data within a predetermined time. The skills of a good interviewer are similar to those of a good actor.

In spite of valiant efforts to ensure that all participants are aware of the purposes of the evaluation and the role of the evaluator, some will be less willing than others to talk to the interviewer. Since interviewees cannot be coerced to submit information, the cooperative ones will provide most of the information. The effect of this on the reliability and validity of data should be considered. Although one cannot predict who will be cooperative, some general cautions can be made. Those on the fringes may be more willing to criticize the program or the organization. Indeed, it could well be that senior administrators and those involved in central activities cannot perceive in any objective way the strengths and the weaknesses of a change because of their more intrinsic involvement in day-to-day operations. Thus, fringe members may be valuable sources of information to the researcher, providing insights not available from more central members. But the researcher should attempt to establish these fringe members' motives for providing such information. Furthermore, the researcher should guard against being identified with deviant or perhaps troublemaking members of the organization. Ability to establish rapport with more established individuals may be jeopardized if the researcher becomes identified with individuals perceived as cynics, rabblerousers, or malcontents. But because they are potentially a valuable source of insightful information, these persons should not be ignored. The reliability of their information should be checked by supplementing it with information from others or directly confronting administrators with the issues. Since fringe members will be in the minority, the weight given to their responses in subsequent analyses should reflect their representation in the organization as a whole.

In the course of an interview, the interviewer must discriminate between factual and objective responses and those primarily expressing attitudes, values, or motives. Formulating questions properly will usually assist in this distinction. If the interviewer wants the interviewee to reconstruct past events, "why" questions should be avoided, since they may promote motivational responses. Questions should instead take a "how" form. If the researcher wishes subjective reactions to events, these should be requested immediately after the interviewee relates the event. Subjective reactions are more richly interpreted if they are embedded in their historical context.

Managing the Data. As the case studies progress, the researcher will become inundated with data. The arrangement of this data quickly becomes a major management problem. Prior to beginning the fieldwork, this problem should be anticipated; a system for creating, storing, and retrieving the data should be ready for implementation.

Procedures for recording data collected in interviews and observations must also be established in advance. A major strategy issue concerns preparation and transformation of these data into readable copy. The researcher basically has two options here. The first is to use portable equipment to make audio or videotape recordings of interviews or observations as they occur. The second option is to take the most complete notes possible during these events and later transform them into written reports. Of course, the researcher can combine these techniques for a third possible option, that is, recording and notetaking.

There are advantages and disadvantages to these various options that must be carefully considered for each case study. Recording provides the most complete and accurate method of preserving the content of interactions. Unless both audio and video recordings can be made, this method is usually not appropriate for observations. It is the more costly option. The equipment is expensive to purchase or rent, and the coding and transformation of the tapes are time-consuming activities. Audio and video recordings very quickly produce a large amount of data, much of which may not be relevant. The investigator then confronts the problem of transforming the recorded data into a condensed and shareable report. Nevertheless, recording does provide a more complete account; and in some cases, it may be warranted, depending on the substantive focus of the inquiry.

Although less expensive, the second option, taking field notes, is subject to biases due to selection and recall. The researcher rarely is able to write down everything that happens. For the most part, he or she notes the most important or salient points. A particularly good interviewee may provide important information so rapidly or observed events may occur so quickly that the researcher has difficulty noting all the important issues.

From one perspective, all data collection, reduction, and analysis activities involve continuously selecting and synthesizing information about organizational behavior. Investigators are confronted with the problem of the optimal point in the life cycle of a case study for selecting and synthesizing. It is not possible to specify a general set of procedures for all organizational case studies, but the researcher must guard against synthesizing data collected in the field before it is known exactly what information will be most relevant for the study. If done too soon, perspectives or data may be lost because the researcher is not yet aware that a topic is important or that data can be collected in a particular area. The researcher must continually exercise caution with respect to data selection and synthesis.

Audio and visual recording selects all activities within range of the equipment. Notetaking starts the process of abstracting earlier.

Subsequent data reduction and analysis further select and abstract from the raw or original data. Delaying the selection preserves more of the information for subsequent referral by the investigator or others. But such delays run up project costs considerably. Therefore, the decision of how to record field data must carefully weigh considerations of the degree of complete recording of all possible events against available resources.

If notes are taken, it is important to transcribe them as soon as possible after completing the interview or observation. The longer one waits, the more details one forgets, thereby introducing another source of bias. We have found it useful to take notes during an interview and then tape-record a summary based upon them. If the summary is dictated, transcribed, and typed as soon as possible, the interviewer will have an opportunity to review the transcript and make any corrections or additions before he or she forgets too many details.

It is impossible to specify a general-purpose filing system for data collected during organizational case studies. The particular substantive focus of the investigation as well as the nature of the organization will suggest an appropriate strategy. The filing system could use as a guiding structure the five previously mentioned dimensions. Alternatively, the data might be arranged by different organizational departments or the different functions accomplished by the organizations. There may also be a series of theoretical issues (such as communication patterns, authority relationships, or boundary maintenance) around which the files could be organized. To facilitate data management, the filing system should be established before data collection begins. However, the researcher should remain flexible enough to modify or adjust the filing system if it becomes clear that a more optimal system for storing and retrieving the information should be adopted.

Analyzing the Data

The discussion thus far has suggested a number of techniques that allow the researcher to sharpen the focus of the investigation throughout the planning and data collection phases of the case studies. The research team that follows these suggestions will have accumulated a vast array of rich and complex data describing organizational structure and function. Its final task is further to collapse and compile this data in order to delineate the major outcomes of the program.

Unfortunately, our suggestions on data analysis are not as specific as those presented in prior sections. This lack of specificity corresponds with most of the social science research literature describing case studies, for it is in analysis that the case study is weakest and needs further development. We take up three interrelated topics. The first concerns validity and reliability in data collection. The second addresses the complex issue of causal explanation in social science research in general and comparative case studies in particular. Third, we discuss briefly an analytical methodology with the potential of providing additional rigor in synthesizing the data collected in comparative case studies.

Validity and Reliability. One of the major methodological problems confronting case studies is the relationship of the data collected and analyzed by the researcher to the "real world" of the structure and functioning of the organization. Through the variety of data collection activities already discussed, the investigator abstracts information characterizing the organization. The process of abstraction is complex, and we do not yet have a system for thoroughly documenting it. Consequently, one must always be concerned with data validity and reliability. *Validity* refers to the degree of accuracy or correctness of the data as a description of a corresponding phenomenon or event. *Reliability* refers to the extent to which the data collection procedures could be repeated and produce the same results.

The data collected in comparative case studies are subject to serious questioning with respect to both validity and reliability. In experiments, surveys, and simulations, a wide variety of sampling and measurement techniques is available for addressing these questions. But in case studies, such techniques have not yet been developed. We have been very concerned with these questions in our work. Our general strategy has been to provide an overall framework for our data collection and analysis, narrow our focus as much as possible, and provide thorough documentation about our procedures. In addition, we include no datum in our analysis unless it can be verified from two independent sources. Nevertheless, if two other social scientists repeated our work, they would likely produce a different set of results. The heart of the dilemma is *replication,* a fundamental requirement of the accumulation of all scientific knowledge.

The organizational case studies produced over the past three decades have produced enormous amounts of detailed data as well as insights relevant to the development of a more general and comprehensive theoretical framework. But, unfortunately, each study essentially stands alone; there has been very little accumulation of knowledge. In our view, this lack of accumulation is attributable to the fact that case study findings are so heavily dependent upon a number of interdependent factors, including the validity and reliability of the data, the disciplinary perspectives of the investigators, and the time-bound nature of cross-sectional studies. The operational definitions implied by the five dimensions we have suggested provide one potential means of more systematically addressing the questions of replication and accumulation in case studies.

A second approach to these data problems is inherent in the design of comparative case studies. When conducting comparative studies, one must employ similar data collection procedures to ensure comparability of data across the organizations. In essence, the comparative design is a replication of the case study in each of the organizations. It is not sufficient for an investigator to produce a number of independent case studies in the comparative design. There must be a common focus on the outcomes of planned social change, and the comparative design builds into all research activities an attempt to achieve uniformity in data collection and analysis procedures.

Causal Analysis. Social scientists generally agree that three factors are necessary for adequate causal explanations: concomitant variation, time order of occurrence, and elimination of all other possible causal explanations. *Concomitant variation* means that if one is trying to establish that variable x, the causal or the independent variable, causes variable y, the effect or the dependent variable, x and y must always occur or vary together. *Time order of occurrence* means variable x must always precede variable y.

These two conditions are not difficult to attain in most social science research designs, including case studies. But the problem in all causal analysis is the third factor, that is, elimination of all other possible causal explanations or variables. In experiments and simulations, one can "control" for other possible causal variables through randomization or other design features. In survey research, one can approach this problem by including a large number of causal variables in a multivariate analysis. But in case studies, it is exceedingly difficult, if not impossible, to eliminate all other causal factors.

Case studies record structure and function in real-life settings, and only through rigorous and documented deductions can one begin to eliminate other causal factors. The comparative case study approach provides some assistance. For example, if it is plausible that five different independent variables could influence an outcome, institutions included in the sample should be chosen to provide variation on the potentially important independent variables.

Network Analysis. The case study methodology is sorely in need of a set of procedures that ensures more systematic data collection and analysis. Unless progress is made in this area, case studies, whether single or comparative, are unlikely to produce an accumulation of knowledge relevant to theory building. The five dimensions proposed provide an agenda for methodological development with this end in mind. Each is described in terms of both structure and process. Structure refers to tasks, functions, decision points, fiscal resources, and personnel. Process implies a set of interconnections among these various units, connections suggesting operational definitions of interrelationships within organizations.

Case studies can be designed to provide specific operational definitions of these networks for each of the five dimensions. For example, the information dimension, which describes the organization as a network of decision points connected via data channels, could be operationally defined by monitoring the flow of information relevant to a particular design throughout the organization. One should follow the paths of information through both the formal and informal channels. These data could then be used to construct a sociogram showing the interrelationships among various information producers, transmitters, and consumers throughout the organization.

Various graph theory and other combinatory techniques need to be developed for characterizing and reducing these networks. The network approach also allows an investigator to consider developing hypotheses concerning the character and nature of networks. Empirical data could then be collected in case studies and "goodness-of-fit" tests applied to compare obtained and theoretically constructed networks. There is a great deal of work to be done in further refining the data collection methods appropriate for each of the five dimensions. But this approach could provide much more systematic methods of data collection, reduction, and analysis in case studies.

Changing Organizations

All organizations are constantly undergoing some kind of transformation, and the rate of change varies across different organizations and over time. But organization management frequently attempts to bring about planned social change to accomplish a specific goal or set of goals (reduce costs, improve services, raise productivity, accomplish new tasks, and the like). These planned interventions always produce unanticipated consequences. It is in the assessment of planned social change that comparative case studies can be most enlightening, for the comprehensive and in-depth data collection procedures produce a vast and rich array of information that sheds light on the latent manifestations of the change activities.

The comparative case study methods we have suggested are very sensitive techniques for uncovering changes in task assignments, functional interrelationships, communication patterns, resource allocation, and interpersonal interactions. All these dimensions are characteristic of collectivities, and thus they are not amenable to investigation using the techniques applicable to the study of change at the individual level. Experiments and surveys, which typically provide uniform stimuli to subjects or respondents, are particularly insensitive to change at the collectivity level. Use of the comparative case study design can contribute significantly to our understanding of the dynamics of change among organizations.

References

Anderson, S. B., and Ball, S. *The Profession and Practice of Program Evaluation*. San Francisco: Jossey-Bass, 1978.

Jahoda, M., and others. *Research Methods in Social Relations*. New York: Holt-Dryden, 1959.

March, J. C. *Handbook of Organizations*. New York: Rand McNally, 1965.

Nielen, G. C. "Foundations for a Curriculum in 'Large Systems.'" In R. A. Buckingham (Ed.), *Education and Large Information Systems*. Amsterdam: North Holland Publishing Company, 1977.

Hugh F. Cline is a senior research sociologist and
Loraine T. Sinnott is an associate research psychgologist
at Educational Testing Service. They are currently
conducting research on the impact of technology
on academic libraries.

A program can be evaluated, and a cost-benefit ratio can be calculated to five decimal places, without ever directly examining outcomes.

The Role of Outcomes in Cost-Benefit Evaluation

Victor Levine

Different evaluation techniques are useful for different kinds of decision making. In deciding which programs should be cut or reduced in the human services sector, where resources are becoming increasingly scarce, it is reasonable to expect that evaluations will employ cost-benefit techniques. The range of outcomes produced in human services programs is immense. While program evaluators from different disciplines can generally agree about what activities a program involves, there is often not consensus concerning what the program's "outcomes" are.

For a point of reference, I have borrowed a definition from Ellis Page, who describes an outcome as "a change in the behaviors and abilities of [an] individual" (1973, p. 159). I will argue that decisions about program cuts should not be based on measures of outcomes alone. What is required is a systematic procedure for comparing the cost of producing outcomes to the value of a "stream of services" that these out-

The author wishes to thank Scarvia Anderson, Samuel Ball, William Garner, and Peter Moock for their helpful comments on an earlier draft of this chapter. The opinions expressed herein (as well as any remaining oversights) are, of course, those of the author.

comes yield over time. Cost-benefit analysis provides such a procedure. Much of this chapter is devoted to examining the difficulties involved in estimating this relationship. Because human service outcomes cover a broad range of areas, good data are often difficult to obtain. The strength of the cost-benefit approach is that it provides a unifying paradigm for identifying the needed data. Even when weak proxies must be substituted for (unavailable) direct measures, the evaluator will at least be able to identify the full range of information that a considered decision should include.

The general topic of applying cost-benefit techniques to human services programs has received extensive discussion (see Mishan, 1975; Rivlin, 1971). Several recent works describe the mechanics of conducting such analyses (Dasgupta, Sen, and Marglin, 1972; Gittinger, 1972; Roemer and Stern, 1975; Squire and van der Tak, 1975). My goal in this chapter is not to examine cost-benefit analysis per se; rather, I am interested in the economist's concept of outcomes as he or she enters the assessment process. Much of the theoretical foundation of cost-benefit analysis comes directly from the theory of the firm. We must, therefore, look at how human services outcomes are similar to firm-produced outputs and the extent to which human services programs operate like firms. My ultimate interest is how and where the evaluator's perception of outcomes fits into the decision-making process.

The director of a human services agency faced with a reduction in total resources must review the available set of program options and decide which to cut back. In many ways, this decision is like that of a firm manager who must make decisions about closing some of the firm's production units, which I call "factories." I will use this program-factory analogy to explore the basic similarities and dissimilarities in the two decision processes. I am particularly interested in the factory equivalent of program outcomes and the place of outcomes in the overall decision-related analysis.

Decision Making Within the Firm

Profit Maximization. Economic theory suggests that the manager of a firm will make decisions with the objective of maximizing the firm's profits (see any standard microeconomics text, such as Henderson and Quandt, 1971). Following my program-factory analogy, imagine a manager who has a number of different factories, each of which produces a different product. In order to maximize profits, two conditions must be met. Within each factory, outputs must be produced in an efficient manner. Among factories, decisions about the output level must be based on the cost of producing outputs and on their value.

Efficient Production. Production processes are defined by the relationship between *inputs* (for example, materials, labor, machinery) and *outputs* (that is, what is produced). A production process is said to be efficient when the maximum amount of output possible is derived from each dollar of inputs. When considering these production relationships, economists distinguish between two principal aspects of efficiency: *technical efficiency* and *allocative efficiency*.

A production process is said to be technically efficient if no more output can be produced, given the same set of physical inputs, by changing the way they are combined. The basic concept relates to a technical or engineering relationship. For example, if some factory were using dump trucks to whisk executives around the production floor and a golf cart to dispose of waste, one might expect total production to increase if the same inputs (truck and cart) were used differently. If an educational program had teachers erasing blackboards while teaching aides gave instruction, one might again expect output to increase if the same inputs (teachers and aides) were utilized differently.

In order to determine if a production process is technically efficient, one must know what the inputs are and how much of each input is consumed and what the outputs are and how much of each output is produced. A technically efficient process is one that attains maximum possible output, given inputs. Of course, what is possible changes as knowledge grows; a process becomes inefficient when a better process is developed.

While technical efficiency describes maximum physical output given a fixed set of physical inputs, allocative efficiency relates to maximum physical output per dollar value of inputs. Given different production processes that are all technically efficient, a profit-maximizing decision maker would choose the lowest-cost process depending upon the prices of the inputs used. For example, if a teacher could grade six exam papers per hour and a teacher aide could grade only three per hour with the same accuracy, one would base the choice of inputs (teachers or aides) on the relative prices of the two. In this case, if teachers cost more than twice as much per hour as aides, it would be allocatively efficient to choose the production process that utilized aides. In order to tell whether a production process is allocatively efficient, one must know the unit price of each input consumed.

Efficient Investment. Attainment of technical and allocative efficiency does not in itself assure profits; production efficiency indicates only that each unit of output is being produced as cheaply as possible. A manager must still determine whether the value of a unit of output is greater than the cost of all the inputs required for its production. In order to make this determination, the manager must have two additional pieces of information: the sale price of final output and the time required to produce and sell it. If the sale price of output is less than the cost of producing it, it is obviously an unprofitable output. Even when the sale price is higher than the costs, attention must be paid to how long capital is tied up in producing it. Since this capital could be earning interest elsewhere, the real value of output may be less than the sale price.

Economic Efficiency

When each individual firm behaves to maximize its own profit, the overall economy approaches *economic efficiency* and societal economic welfare is maximized. That is, the last dollar allocated to producing any specific outcome would not be more productive elsewhere. A microeconomics text will show that, given some assumptions about the free operation of markets, competition among many firms, and free access to information, there can exist an optimal set of answers to questions about which outputs should be produced and the inputs and processes that should be used in their production (see the treatment of equilibrium and welfare in any standard microeconomics text, such as Henderson and Quandt, 1971, chap. 4–7).

While the firm's decision maker need only be concerned with the firm's own profits, the maximization of societal welfare is brought about through market-generated price adjustments. Adam Smith likened these market adjustments to the intervention of an "invisible hand."

Agency Decision Making

Since human services outcomes are generally not produced or traded competitively, responsibility for their production falls to the public sector. In the absence of such competition and markets, the burden for making decisions falls to the decision maker in the public sector. The principal purpose of cost-benefit evaluation is to provide this decision maker with information that compensates for the missing signals that come from prices in the competitive market. The social service decision maker must, in addition to making the decisions of the firm manager, incorporate a broader perspective into decision-making activities. In a sense, he or she must be both the manager of the enterprise and the invisible hand.

In program evaluation, a distinction is commonly made between formative and summative evaluation. This dichotomy is analogous to the production and investment components of economic efficiency already described. *Formative evaluation* looks at process and production relationships. *Summative evaluation* looks at the relationship between the value of physical inputs and the value of outcomes. Cost-benefit evaluation is a form of summative evaluation and is the technique suitable of making immediate decisions about program cuts.

In order to estimate the value of outcomes that carry no observable market price, it is important to consider the nature of these outcomes. Human services programs operate in an extremely broad range of areas: Some programs are intended to achieve a single objective (for example, curing drug addiction or providing career counseling); other programs have fairly broad objectives and are seen as affecting a client throughout his or her lifetime. If there is a common denominator that characterizes programs in this sector, it is that they change the program participants. By and large, the programs are interventions; individuals enter these programs and, some time later, they leave changed. A program is like a factory to which some item has been brought for modification or repair; human services programs are unique in that the item to be repaired is a person rather than an appliance. The essence of human services program outcomes is change in individuals.

Consumption Goods and Capital Goods. If one defines *outcomes* in this context as changes in program participants and *benefits* as the value of these changes, one must consider how changes in individuals can be of value. Economists refer to desirable outcomes as *goods,* which they divide into consumption and capital categories. *Consumption goods* are used up in a short time. The value of capital goods lies in their usefulness in producing other goods and services over time; they are like tools. Since human services programs change participants and their effects persist long after the client has completed participation, program outcomes can be seen as capital goods. Their value is derived from the value of the stream of services they will yield over the client's lifetime. Like tools, the value of their services depends on how, where, and for how long the tools will be used. When such tools are freely traded in open markets (as is the case for lathes and tractors), the observed sale price will equal the time-adjusted value of this stream of services.

Human Capital. Human services outcomes are different from physical capital in one essential way: They are embodied in the program participants. While they provide services to the individual over a long time (and are therefore capital goods), human services outcomes cannot be bought and sold because they are an inseparable part of the participants. Since these outcomes are embodied in human beings, they are often termed *human capital.* This embodiment complicates the process of estimating the value of outcomes. In the absence of market prices, the projected value of services must be used to impute a price to these outcomes. This concept of human capital has received substantial consideration over the past two decades (see, for example, Becker, 1975; Schultz, 1972) and has been applied to many forms of investment that change individual productivity, including education (Schultz, 1963; Weisbrod, 1962), health (Grossman, 1972), migration (Sjaastad, 1962), training on the job (Mincer, 1974), and job search (Stigler, 1962).

In order to estimate the full value of program outcomes, it is useful to consider the possible range of these services. One might, for example, divide these services up into three broad categories: market production, nonmarket production, and externalities. The most obvious type of service (and the one that has received the greatest attention in cost-benefit evaluations) is change in the individual participant's productivity in the marketplace. One reason for this emphasis is that change in market productivity is the least difficult to estimate, although this process is fraught with certain ambiguities. A second type of service is change in participant productivity *outside* the marketplace. There is evidence to suggest that human services program outcomes make individuals more productive in managing their daily lives in general and in specific activities such as shopping, child rearing, and producing family health (Terleckyj, 1976). The area of nonmarket production has received considerable attention in the past ten years (see Moock, 1974, on the impact of education on household production). These benefits are often omitted from program analyses because they are substantially more difficult to observe and are particularly difficult to price.

A third type of benefit, often called *externalities,* is enjoyed by members of society other than the program participants. In certain programs (for example, antirecidivism, drug counseling, and contagious disease control), it is clear that a very substantial share of total benefits may take the form of externalities. It has been argued that there are substantial externalities to many programs that are principally participant-oriented (see Mishan, 1971).

The three categories I have created are by no means exhaustive, nor is this the only system that could be used for conceptually organizing outcome-related services. For example, benefits accruing to children because a program produces better parents could be classed as either nonmarket production or as externalities. Similarly, the positive impact of program outcomes on the enjoyment of leisure time could be counted either as a form of household production (see Becker, 1965) or could be placed in an entirely separate fourth category. The point here is simply that there is a wide range of benefits attributable to program outcomes, and if only marketed benefits are included, the program evaluation can be substantially distorted. Estimating the value of outcomes requires specifying the full range of services, the timing of their occurrence, and the "price" that should be attached to each.

The aggregate value of these services over the program participants' lifetimes (adjusted for time) is conceptually equal to the "sale price" of program outcomes. Consideration of how program evaluators estimate the value of such services will dominate the last half of this chapter.

Program Costs. Given an estimate of program benefits, the investment character of the program remains unidentified until the cost of producing outcomes is defined. From a social perspective, the cost of any input is its value in its best alternative use. All costs are viewed as "opportunity costs" because by using an input in any specific way, the possibility of using it elsewhere is forgone. In defining the costs of producing social services outcomes, the evaluator must determine what resources are being used and what they would be worth elsewhere. For most inputs, the process is fairly straightforward. A program's budget generally provides accurate data on the quantities and prices of purchased inputs. Other program inputs, such as program participants' own time, are more problematic. In many cases, it is difficult to decide exactly how this time should be valued. Even with certain purchased inputs, the observed purchase price does not necessarily provide a good estimate of value elsewhere. For example, the salaries paid to public employees need not reflect their productivity in the private sector. I shall explore this question of the divergence of market prices from opportunity costs in more detail later in the chapter.

Given data on the price and timing of program inputs and the value and timing of outcome services, these data can be summarized in a decision-oriented statistic. Estimating this statistic (which contrasts the value of all inputs with the value of all outcomes) requires adjusting for differences in the time at which costs and benefits occur. This adjustment can be made through use of the standard discounting identity (see Henderson and Quandt, 1971, chap. 8):

$$PV = \frac{FV}{(1 + r)^t} \tag{1}$$

In this identity, the present value (*PV*) describes how much a future payment (*FV*) is worth today based on the knowledge that the payment will be received after *t* years with compound discounting at rate *r*. The concept answers the question "How much money would have to be deposited in a savings account today (*PV*) so that after *t* years, given a compound interest rate of *r*, there would be a specific amount of money (*FV*) in the account?"

Inspection of the discounting identity shows that the greater the value of either *t* or *r*, the smaller the present value (PV) of any future payment. Over long periods of time, the effects of discounting can be substantial. For example, the present value of a payment of $300 in twenty years is worth less than $30 (*PV*) when discounted at 10 percent.

Once all the cost and benefit items have been discounted to a common point in time, the investment character of a program outcome can be described in any one of several summary statistics. The *net present value* (*NPV*) is simply the discounted value of all benefits minus the discounted value of all costs. Profitable investments are characterized by *NPV*s that are greater than zero. The *cost-benefit* ratio (*C-B*) is the discounted value of costs divided by the discounted value of benefits. A profitable investment will have a *C-B* ratio of less than one.

A third summary statistic, called the *internal rate of return* (*IRR*), is the discount rate at which the *NPV* equals zero and the *C-B* ratio equals 1.0. In most human services programs, there will be a unique *IRR* that satisfies these conditions. Profitable investments are those for which the *IRR* is higher than the interest cost of financing the program. When one is evaluating different programs that are not mutually exclusive, any of the three summary statistics will generally provide the same decision-related signals. These summary statistics can be constructed to reflect either the investment characteristic of producing one more unit of outcomes (that is, the *marginal* unit) or the *average* investment characteristics of the program generally.

Perspective of the Evaluation. At the level of the firm, decision makers are concerned with the impact of any decision on firm profits. Social service decision making is considerably more complex. In addition to the question of externalities already raised, the social decision maker must ask which members of society will bear specific costs and who will be the recipients of benefits. Obviously, a social agency cannot be interested in minimizing government cost in a manner analogous to the firm. From a government perspective, it is not clear what the analogue of firm profits would be.

Economists generally distinguish between two principal perspectives from which outcomes can be evaluated: the social perspective and the private perspective. From the social perspective, any resource devoted to a program that any member of society could productively use elsewhere is counted as a program cost. Similarly, any benefit accruing to any member of society is included among the total benefits. This perspective is directed at maximizing the size of the overall societal pie without attention to the size of individual slices.

When outcomes are evaluated from the private perspective, only those costs borne by program participants are included as costs, and only those benefits (net of taxes) that accrue directly to the participant are included in the calculation of the total benefits. For example, in a government-sponsored vocational training program, the cost of instructors' salaries and fringe benefits, rent, heat, books, and materials would be counted as social costs but not as private costs. Items such as the opportunity cost of participants' time, extra expenses for travel, lunches, or housing borne by the participants would be private costs *and* social costs (since the participants are members of society). Transfers between the program and the participants (for example, tuition, fees, or living stipends) would affect the private rate of return but not the social rate of return because they are really transfers of resources *between* society members and do not represent a net gain or loss to society in general.

While social and private perspectives represent the theoretical poles from which any program can be evaluated, actual decision making often occurs within a more limited framework. Specific programs are developed and evaluated by agencies that operate within a well-specified and limited mandate. It is frequently impractical to ask how a program affects society; individual programs are compared to one another in terms of how well each fulfills the agency mandate. Large-scale projects such as dams and highways may warrant analysis from a broad social perspective, but incorporation of this approach into small programs is not always feasible.

The question of perspective becomes further complicated when outcomes are targeted toward special population groups. From the social perspective, efficiency requires maximizing *total* benefit, and it is generally recognized that there is a loss in efficiency when redistributional objectives are included in a program's design. Human services programs typically are targeted; while an agency mandate may specify the nature of this targeting, it will not (for obvious political reasons) specify the rate at which particular populations groups should be preferred. Arthur Okun (1975) has described this issue as an efficiency-equity trade-off. Redistributional objectives substantially complicate the analysis process.

To summarize, I began by suggesting that the outcomes of social programs should be thought of as the changes these programs induce in the participants and that each program could be thought of as resembling a small factory that utilized a particular production process in which inputs were consumed and outcomes were produced. The production process could be inefficient in either of two ways. Technical inefficiency would mean that, given the physical resources allocated to the process, less than the maximum possible physical output was being produced. Allocative inefficiency would mean that more output per dollar cost could be produced by substituting relatively less expensive (but equally productive) inputs for more expensive inputs.

While these two types of efficiency relate to the production process, I have shown it is possible to describe the investment character of producing outcomes (given the production processes as they exist) by comparing the discounted present value of costs to the discounted present value of the services the outcomes will yield. Costs are thought of as opportunity costs, and while observed market prices are often a good indication of cost, adjustments are needed for many inputs. Since program outcomes (the changes that occur in program participants) are embodied in the participants, they have no observable market prices. A price must be imputed by estimating the discounted value of the services they will yield (both in and out of the labor market) over the participants' lifetimes. The discounted value of this stream of services is conceptually the price at which these outcomes would be traded if such trading were possible.

I have considered how, once identified, these data on costs and benefits could be summarized in a single term that describes the investment characteristics of the program. Finally, I have considered the distribution of costs and benefits among different members of society, distinguishing between the social rate of return and the private rate of return.

Data Limitations

Having described the concepts underlying the economic evaluation of social services outcomes, I now consider the data limitations under which such decision making occurs. Through use of the firm-agency metaphor, I compare social decision making to the market model from which the basic concepts evolved.

Direct Costs. First there is the question of how program costs are actually estimated. From an economic perspective, all costs are opportunity costs. Many program inputs do have observable market prices, and in most cases, these prices are accepted as a reasonable measure of economic cost. Aside from the opportunity cost of participants' time, which I will examine more closely later, valuing the cost of program staff time is the major problem area. To the extent that inputs are interchangeable in many processes, their observed market prices are likely to reflect economic costs. Underpriced inputs (unit price lower than the value of marginal productivity) will be in demand in many processes. Purchasers will compete for the available stocks and bid up the price of the input. Similarly, overpriced inputs will be shunned and their prices will fall. Most human services outcomes are produced in the public sector, and there is a fundamental question about the extent to which salaries respond to market pressures and therefore reflect productivity. Many inputs used in both the public and market sectors (for example, motor vehicles and stationery supplies) are completely interchangeable between sectors. While there is some mobility in and out of public employment, government salaries tend to be set by administrative rather than market practices, and the economic cost of these inputs may be poorly represented by observed wages. This problem is intensified in economies where the government sector dominates the employment of specific types of labor, such as university graduates.

Whenever possible, economists tend to rely on observed market prices as the preferred measure of the best alternative value of program inputs. This approach is useful so long as these inputs have recognizable counterparts that are marketed. While office equipment, fuel, and utilities are widely bought and sold (and their market price can be taken as indicative of the value of their contribution everywhere), difficulties arise when some inputs are more or less specific to the production of a particular set of outcomes. For example, a particular curricular aid might be very important in an educational program and virtually useless elsewhere. Since there is little competition among firms that would use this input, there is no market mechanism to assure that its contribution to output would really be equal to its cost. The observed price of this input might be substantially different from its economic cost to society. The problem intensifies when one considers the price of staff inputs. Although there may be an observable budget figure for salaries and fringe benefits, it is not always clear that this represents the economic cost of time used. As staff requirements become more program-specific, estimation of economic costs becomes more difficult.

Participants' Time. Estimation of the economic costs of participants' time is even more problematic. When participants are taking part in a human services program that precludes working for money elsewhere, the value of their time spent elsewhere is not directly observable. A "shadow wage" can be imputed to their time inputs in a variety of ways. For example, their observed wage prior to entry, or that of a "matched" contrast group, could be used as a proxy for what they might have been earning. If an individual was unemployed, imprisoned, or disabled, prior observation of wages is precluded. Moreover, even when prior wage data are available, it is not always clear that the old job is indicative of present and future opportunities. An individual might enter a program in response to a plant closing or a layoff. When one uses prior observations, one implicitly assumes that, in the absence of the program, the participant would continue to do exactly what he or she was doing before.

Wages versus Productivity. Even when the assumption that a specified wage would be earned seems supportable, there are still problems in using the prior wage as a measure of opportunity cost of a participant's time inputs. First, if the weekly hours devoted to the program differ from previous hours worked, should the previous weekly wage rate or the hourly rate multiplied by actual program hours be used? If the former measure (weekly wage rate) is used, a zero value is implicitly attached to time spent in home production or leisure activities. If the latter is used, it can be argued that opportunity cost is understated. Finally, even if one assumes that compensation reflects marginal productivity, there is still the question of how adequately observed wages reflect the full compensation package. Certain adjustments must be made.

One obvious adjustment is for the nonmoney component of the compensation package made up of items such as vacation, medical insurance, and retirement benefits. These nonmoney benefits represent an important part of full compensation and vary substantially by industry and by firm within industry. With some amount of research, their value can usually be estimated. Excluding these items can seriously bias estimates of economic cost derived from wage data. There are other nonpecuniary aspects of work that are more difficult to price but that may also be important. For example, one would expect wages to be influenced by the pleasantness or dangerousness of the work location. As marginal tax rates rise with average earnings, there are incentives for the nonwage portion of the compensation package to increase.

Another intangible but very important component of the compensation package is on-the-job training that may be occurring at the workplace. The shape of the typical age-earnings profile suggests that substantial changes in individual productivity occur over the working lifetime. Many economists attribute these changes to learning that occurs on the job (Becker, 1975; Ben-Porath, 1967; Mincer, 1974) and argue that this training forms an important part of the total compensation package. Firms are seen as providing both wages and training; individuals are seen as forgoing some wages to receive additional training. The importance of this part of the compensation package is substantial and has been estimated to be as high as 50 percent of observed money earnings at the beginning of the working lifetime (Lazear, 1976). Failure to include this nonmonetary training component in the estimation of compensation can distort program evaluations (Levine, 1979); yet the precise nature of this on-the-job training component is far from resolved (see Cain, 1976, on alternative theories).

Control Groups. When direct measures of participants' wages prior to program entry are unavailable, estimates can be developed by observing "matched" groups. The difficulty in this approach is that when participants self-select in human services programs (as is almost universally the case), perfectly matched control groups do not exist by definition. No matter how carefully members are selected or how comprehensive the matching criteria, some unobserved variable exists that is perfectly correlated with the participation decision.

Estimating Benefits. As with costs, the cost-benefit criterion requires that the value of outcomes be summarized in a single benefit figure. As noted, the greatest imprecision in the cost estimate involves making inferences about (unobserved) productivity losses. In general, the larger the proportion of total cost that is made up of opportunity cost of participants' time, the larger the margin for error in the overall cost estimate. On the benefits side, this fundamental problem of estimating unobserved productivity becomes even more critical. Most evaluations concentrate on changes in market productivity as the principal benefit that can be attributed to program outcomes. I defined outcomes as the change in the individual and benefits as the value of services attributable to this change. While one might be able to estimate the total value of an individual's market service at one point, deciding what part of this total should be attributed uniquely to a given program is extremely difficult. Such an estimate requires first estimating what total services would have been in the absence of the program. The unique contribution of the outcomes can only be estimated as the difference between observed services (given the program) and assumed services (without the program). While estimates based on these unobserved data constitute only part of the total cost estimate, they are likely to constitute all of the benefits estimate, protests about the importance of nonmarket productivity notwithstanding.

There are also differences in the length of time over which these projections must be made in comparing cost and benefit estimates. Typically, social service treatments last no more than several years, while the outcomes persist over participants' working lifetimes (or beyond). This difference in duration can affect the accuracy of estimates in several ways. First, the need for immediate decisions precludes lifetime observation. While, for example, it is not unusual to follow a control group through the duration of a program in order to estimate opportunity costs, it would not be feasible to follow group members throughout their entire lifetimes. The benefits estimate must be based on a proportionately smaller data base. Moreover, to the extent that there are life cycle patterns to productivity that relate to individual maturation, experience, and other factors, such changes are likely to be much less important over the course of the program than over the entire life cycle. Similarly, to the extent that secular changes in the economy have a different impact on different kinds of human capital, these effects may have a minimal impact in the short run, while they may have a substantial effect over a lifetime. Of course, as can be seen in the discounting identity, the relative importance of distant events may be small in the overall benefit estimate. Nonetheless, the long range over which such estimates must be made makes them much more susceptible to error.

Nonmarket Benefits. Estimating the value of nonmarket changes in individual productivity is even more difficult. Not only must inferences be made about what such productivity would have been without the program, but productivity, given the program, is itself difficult to estimate. Relatively little is known about production away from work, and it is therefore not surprising that these benefits, while acknowledged as being important, are rarely included.

Focusing on Outcomes Directly

Direct Measures. Clearly, imputing a value to program outcomes based on data about the services these outcomes produce is indirect and problematic. It might be tempting to approach the benefit question by measuring outcomes directly (that is, changes in program participants) and using some price index to calculate the value of benefits. Many outcomes do lend themselves to direct measurement, and tests are frequently administered to program participants before and after participation to gauge changes. While such data are useful in examining production efficiency (about which more follows), they do not provide much useful information about the investment characteristics of such programs.

To begin with, social service programs tend to induce changes in a wide spectrum of areas. The instruments used to measure these changes typically capture only a small part of the total change; it is often argued that what is captured represents the total package. For example, changes in reading and math achievement are frequently used to indicate overall learning. So long as other aspects of the educational experience tend to occur in fixed proportion to changes in math and reading, such measures can be used as proxies for the overall outcome package. There is, however, no guarantee that such fixed relationships exist. In fact, it may be that other important outcomes accompany *lower* levels of gain in reading and math, specifically because resources have been diverted to their production.

Units. Even if there were accurate measurement of all relevant program outcomes, there would still be difficulties in combining such information to generate an aggregate benefit measure. Most instruments for measuring outcomes do not employ an interval scale. Even if there were an empirical base from which one could estimate the true value of a specific unit of some outcome, there would be no reason to believe another unit would represent the same "amount" of outcome. Even if all units represented equal amounts of outcome, one would still expect different units to have different "prices." In some cases, a minimum level of some outcome might be essential for the outcome to have any value. Eventually, one would expect there to be diminishing returns to marginal units of any outcome. One would certainly not expect a linear relationship to exist between quantities and values, however measured.

The discounting identity (Equation 1) shows that the same output would vary in value depending upon the time it occurred, and I have already mentioned that the value attached to producing an outcome may depend upon the specific subpopulation that enjoys it. The value of a stream of services would depend upon the set of complementary capital (human and physical) with which it was combined. To the extent that different groups vary, on average, in their other attributes and their opportunities (geographic, family contacts, access to finance, and so forth), any specific outcome would produce a set of services that also differed in value. Moreover, in the case of market productivity, value would also depend upon anticipated labor force attachment and hours worked.

For these reasons, summative evaluation of program investment characteristics cannot be based upon direct measurement of outcomes alone. Since services must be measured to estimate benefit value, there is a sense in which measurement of outcomes (as I have defined them) is gratuitous. Evaluators must guard against inferring the existence of outcomes from their estimates of benefits. If outcomes are seen solely as an abstraction linking inputs to benefits, they may be overlooked entirely. A program can be evaluated, and a cost-benefit ratio can be calculated to five decimal places, without ever directly looking at outcomes themselves. Unless process and outcome data are collected, it is dangerous to assume the value of services is really related to program inputs. These (process and outcome) data are critical, although they do not enter directly in calculating the summary statistic (Equation 1).

In practice, what really is measured is often *participation,* not outcomes. A group of individuals that has participated in a human services program is later found to have different average earnings (or incidence of unemployment, drug addiction, criminal conviction, mortality, or whatever) than a "similar" group. These differences in group experience are chosen as the focus of the evaluation for two reasons. First, they are more readily measured than the changes that induce them. Second, they can be more readily "priced." Unfortunately, when one applies this approach, the program and the program outcomes become almost synonymous.

Dangers of Generalization. While the distinction between program and outcomes may seem unimportant in estimating cost-benefit ratio, failure to recognize that there are differences can have important, and potentially dangerous, implications if the results of specific evaluations are generalized. At the beginning of this chapter, I noted that cost-benefit analysis is the appropriate technique for making decisions about program cuts. If, for example, there were only two program options (1 and 2) that produced outcomes A and B, respectively, cost-benefit evaluations of both programs would be helpful in choosing between them. If program 1 were found to have a higher *C-B* ratio than program 2, a decision to reduce the production of outcome A would be warranted. While this decision would be correct given the two production processes (1 and 2), it would provide no general information about the relative desirability of producing A or B elsewhere in the future. Cost-benefit analysis, as I have described it, is a method for systematically describing the investment character of a set of outcomes produced in a specific way, using specific inputs, serving specific clients, in a particular setting. In my example, outcome A may have been found to be a poor investment because the program was wastefully managed or because unnecessarily costly inputs were used, although less expensive substitutes existed. Similarly, if outcome A were produced in different clients (younger, older, urban, and so forth), it might have proved to be a better investment. While the point may seem self-evident, there is an ever-present danger of using cost-benefit evaluations of one program as a basis for eliminating another, even when both programs ostensibly produce the same outcomes.

The resource crunch now faced by the human services sector will require making difficult decisions. Research that results in good decisions about which outcomes to reduce today may leave a legacy of misinformation about which outcomes should be preferred tomorrow. While *C-B* analysis is a good technique for answering a specific kind of question, it does not automatically provide information that can be generalized to making broad statements about outcomes per se.

This chapter has reviewed the role of outcomes in economic evaluations that use the cost-benefit approach. I have shown that, while *C-B* analysis is useful for looking at the investment characteristics of producing outcome alternatives given the way these outcomes are produced, findings cannot be generalized beyond the specific program under consideration. Moreover, I have shown that the process of *C-B* itself involves data limitations and ambiguities. Perhaps the best way to review the place of outcomes in the *C-B* approach is through reapplication of the program-factory metaphor.

Picture a social service decision maker faced with a set of outcome factories. He or she has a reasonably good idea what inputs each factory uses (meausured in physical units) but may not know the appropriate prices for them all. Although the factories have names, it is not always clear what they produce. Basically, they are in the business of repairing or improving machines. Individuals who own these machines (program participants) remove them from productive use elsewhere and leave them at the factories (at least for some number of hours each week). Some time later they retrieve these machines from the factory and put them back to work in their principal occupations. The visit to the factory has changed these machines (produced outcomes), but not always in clearly identifiable ways. The value of these changes is the discounted (that is, time-adjusted) value of the extra output these machines can now produce (which is attributable to the visit to the factory). The decision maker does not have a direct measure of production lost while these machines were at the factory nor does he know what they would have gone on to produce had they not visited the factory. Moreover, some of the value of the changes brought about at the factory occurs outside the market sector, often unobserved and always without a direct price. Other benefits due to these changes accrue to individuals other than the machine owners. To further complicate the matter, the decision maker is instructed to attach special value to improvements in machines belonging to particular members of society, but the level of this preference is never explicitly stated. The machines are never bought or sold and have no market price. The decision maker is asked to close some of these factories in a way that minimizes social loss. The decision maker often has no information on the efficiency with which individual factories are run.

Conclusions. I have argued that allocative decisions about the production of human services outcomes should not be based on measures of outcomes alone but should incorporate information on the costs and the value of the services these outcomes yield. Cost-benefit analysis provides a tool for systematically organizing such information, and the evaluative process can provide a summary statistic that is useful in decision making. I have noted that the evaluation process is complex and difficult; much of the difficulty is related to inadequate data.

The second half of the chapter focuses on ways these data problems can limit the reliability of evaluation findings. Not surprisingly, allocative decision making is more difficult in the human services sector than in industry.

On the positive side, the cost-benefit approach provides the evaluator with a framework for identifying the broad range of factors that ought to enter the decision process. Even when weak proxies must be used in place of unavailable data, relevant factors are at least identified. Once data have been collected, evaluators can easily test the sensitivity of their findings to alternative assumptions about the level and value of services that are (at least assumed to be) associated with a particular program. As assumptions change, the estimated summary statistic (Equation 1) can easily be recomputed. The process helps to identify the areas in which better data are needed. As data and research methods improve, cost-benefit analysis will become increasingly valuable as a tool for decision making.

References

Becker, G. S. "A Theory of the Allocation of Time." *The Economic Journal,* 1965, *75* (299), 493–517.

Becker, G. S. *Human Capital.* (2nd ed.) New York: National Bureau of Economic Research (distributed by Columbia University Press), 1975.

Ben-Porath, Y. "The Production of Human Capital and the Lifecycle of Earnings." *Journal of Political Economy,* 1967, *75* (4, part 1), 352–365.

Cain, G. C. "The Challenge of Segmented Labor Market Theories to Orthodox Theory: A Survey." *Journal of Economic Literature,* 1976, *14* (4), 1215–1257.

Dasgupta, P., Sen, A., and Marglin, S. *Guidelines for Project Evaluation.* New York: United Nations Publications, 1972.

Gittinger, J. P. *Economic Analysis of Agricultural Projects.* Baltimore: Johns Hopkins University Press, 1972.

Grossman, M. "On the Concept of Health Capital and the Demand for Health." *Journal of Political Economy,* 1972, *80* (2), 223–255.

Henderson, J. M., and Quandt, R. E. *Microeconomic Theory: A Mathematical Approach.* (2nd ed.) New York: McGraw-Hill, 1971.

Lazear, E. "Age, Experience, and Wage Growth." *American Economic Review,* 1976, *66* (4), 548–1058.

Levine, V. "Evaluating Vocational Training Alternatives Using Single Period Earnings Data: A Technical Note." *Comparative Education Review,* 1979, *23* (1), 125–133.

Mincer, J. *Schooling, Experience and Earnings.* New York: National Bureau of Economic Research (distributed by Columbia University Press), 1974.

Mishan, E. J. "The Postwar Literature on Externalities: An Interpretive Essay." *Journal of Economic Literature,* 1971, *9* (1), 1–28.

Mishan, E. J. *Economics for Social Decisions: Elements of Cost-Benefit Analysis.* New York: Praeger, 1973.

Mishan, E. J. *Cost Benefit Analysis: An Informal Introduction.* (rev. ed.) London: Allen & Unwin, 1975.

Moock, P. R. "Economic Aspects of the Family as Educator." *Teachers College Record,* 1974, *76* (2), 266–278.

Okun, A. M. *Equality and Efficiency: The Big Tradeoff.* Washington, D.C.: The Brookings Institution, 1975.

Page, E. B. "Effects of Higher Education: Outcomes, Values, or Benefits." In S. C. Lewis and J. P. Taubman (Eds.), *Does College Matter?* New York: Academic Press, 1973.

Rivlin, A. M. *Systematic Thought for Social Action.* Washington, D.C.: The Brookings Institution, 1971.

Roemer, M., and Stern, J. J. *The Appraisal of Development Projects: A Practical Guide to Project Analysis with Case Studies and Solutions.* New York: Praeger, 1975.

Schultz, T. W. *The Economic Value of Education.* New York: Columbia University Press, 1963.

Schultz, T. W. *Human Resources.* New York: National Bureau of Economic Research (distributed by Columbia University Press), 1972.

Sjaastad, L. A. "The Costs and Returns to Human Migration." *Journal of Political Economy,* 1962, *70* (5, part 2), 80–94.

Squire, L., and van der Tak, H. G. *Economic Analysis of Projects.* Baltimore: Johns Hopkins University Press, 1975.

Stigler, G. J. "Information in the Labor Market." *Journal of Political Economy,* 1962, *70* (5, part 2), 94–105.

Terleckyj, N. E. (Ed.). *Household Production and Consumption.* New York: National Bureau of Economic Research (distributed by Columbia University Press), 1976.

Weisbrod, B. A. "Education and Investment in Human Capital." *Journal of Political Economy,* 1962, *70* (5, part 2), 106–123.

Victor Levine is a research associate at the Human Resources Center,
The Wharton School, University of Pennsylvania. His area of
specialization is the economics of education, and he conducts
an annual workshop on program evaluation at Educational
Testing Service.

The assessment of the outcomes of social programs should always
include estimates of the size of the effects produced.
Various approaches to this problem are discussed.

Assessing the Effectiveness of Social Programs: Methodological and Conceptual Issues

Lee Sechrest
William E. Yeaton

When an evaluation's major purpose is to shed light on decisions having clear policy implications, it is difficult to imagine a choice regarding the future implementation of programming being made *without* consideration of the magnitude of the effects involved. Some interventions may produce effects that, however regular, are just too small to be of any social importance.

Realistically, there is a host of plausible factors besides effect size that are likely to influence a policy maker's decision about future implementation of programs; political, economic, and ethical issues weigh heavily in the decision-making process. However, faced with research outcomes of ambiguous or even unknown meaning, those charged with responsibility for making decisions can rely only on intuitions, a highly undesirable state of affairs.

Convinced of the importance of estimating the size of effects in research and evaluation, we began systematically to study existing ways of determining effect size (Sechrest and Yeaton, 1979b). We adopted the simple yet robust definition of an effect as the difference between means for two independent groups or conditions. We refined the definition for contingency tables, regression, and correlational analyses, though our simple definition will suffice for purposes of this discussion. A 20 percent difference between experimental and control groups in utilization of health services, a difference in attendance of 10.5 students per day during baseline and treatment conditions, and a salary differential of $1,250 between professional men and women all illustrate this definition of an effect.

Statistical Approaches

Unfortunately, we still lacked any direct information pertaining to the size of the outcome; it was not possible to say whether a 20 percent difference between groups, 10.5 students per day, or $1,250 represented, say, small, medium, or large effects. We turned, with eventual disappointment, to the existing statistical approaches to effect size estimation, namely, measures of proportion of variance accounted for. We have previously reviewed these statistical approaches to the size of experimental (or quasiexperimental) effects (Sechrest and Yeaton, 1979b). The considerations for choosing among the various estimators are numerous, but their shared limitations are worth elaborating upon. All the estimators are biased, and it is impossible to determine the extend of the bias involved. Depending on the circumstances (for example, number of subjects, proportion of error variance present, or kind of ANOVA model chosen), these estimators will tend to produce values that can differ substantially. Speaking in general terms, all suffer the deficiency of depending upon the specific features of the experiment and its implementation. For example, the percentage of variance accounted for by any of these estimators will vary as a function of how much variance is built into the experiment. A relatively homogeneous sample of subjects (for example, college students) would exhibit less variance in the dependent variable than a heterogeneous group (for example, people riding the subway in New York City). It should be easier to account for variance with a homogeneous than a heterogeneous sample. Since most of the estimators are expressed in terms of percentage of variance accounted for, we are in the rather uncomfortable position of estimating the size of an effect where the size depends upon (is confounded by) the choice of sample.

Similarly, the precision used in conducting an experiment would surely produce differing amounts of variance. Treatments implemented by different experimenters at different times of day in different rooms using slightly different cover stories should induce subjects to perform in rather disparate ways. Since mean values of experimental and control groups are not likely to change as a function of this experimental imprecision, experimental effects, as we have defined them, would remain constant. Experienced and inexperienced researchers should produce the same experimental effects but with different variances; hence, statistics estimating effect size will vary markedly. Since all the statistical estimates of effect size are ratio estimators, small changes in variance can greatly alter size of effects expressed in percentage of variance accounted for. Those features of an experiment that influence variance produced will also alter these estimates. For example, the number, strength, and range of treatments are other determinants of the amount of variance available to be accounted for. Effect size estimates will fluctuate as these determinants take on new values. For the same reasons, statistical significance is an inappropriate criterion upon which to gauge the size of an effect.

What then? As Benjamin Franklin said, "Necessity is the mother of invention," and we clearly wanted an offspring. We have begun to develop alternatives to statistical approaches to the effect size estimation problem; an elaboration of these initial efforts appears in a second paper (Sechrest and Yeaton, 1979a). We have considered several empirical approaches for estimating effect size, which we have classified into the broad categories of *judgmental* and *normative*.

Judgmental Approaches. The most common judgmental approach is probably intuitive. A policy maker examines the results of an evaluation, forms some subjective impression of the magnitude of impact, and takes this impression into account when making a policy decision. The impression of effect size the policy maker takes from reading the results of an evaluation may well be based on experience with similar problems using similar interventions. Unfortunately, this experimental background is likely to be different for different persons or even for the same person at different times. Consequently, judges are not apt to agree on their assessments of the magnitudes of an effect. Choose the appropriate judge and you can probably choose any desired answer to the question "How big would you describe this effect to be?"

There are instances, however, where disagreement is much less likely. McSweeny (1978) has reported on the effects of instituting a twenty-cent surcharge for each local directory assistance call per telephone per month (beyond three calls) for telephone subscribers in Cincinnati. The change of approximately sixty thousand calls per day in the experimental series after the charge was introduced is likely to be termed large by even the most conservative judge. The plausibility of the response cost procedure being responsible for the change demonstrated is greatly enhanced by the inclusion of a control series of long-distance directory assistance calls that did not receive the twenty-cent surcharge *or* decrease in frequency. Even without the control series, we are still much more likely to believe the functionality of the procedures, given the absolute change produced in this study. However, if one knew that a simple televised plea to cut down on local directory assistance calls would have decreased their frequency by fifty thousand per day, one would not be as likely to call the obtained decrease of sixty thousand calls a large effect.

We would go so far as to speculate that the production of large effects is on a par with the three factors cited by Cline and Sinnott in this volume as being necessary for adequate causal explanation in case studies. It is decidedly easier to argue away nonpreferred causal explanation in the face of substantial changes in dependent variable responding; small changes allow these rival explanations to become more believable, a point vividly illustrated by the McSweeny case study (assuming, for argument's sake, that the control series was not available).

Some judges are more likely to be convincing than others. Experts are often called upon when they are more informed sources of knowledge. Experts in an area of research and evaluation are more likely to be aware of similar work in the area of interest; in fact, their designation as expert may be owing to this greater awareness. Given the homogeneity of experimental backgrounds of experts in an area, we might expect a good deal of concurrence in their judgments about experimental effects. We have tested this notion, sending descriptions of smoking treatments to experts in the modification of smoking behavior. Judgments of probable success were correlated with reports of actual success reported in the results sections of studies from which the descriptions were taken. The average correlation was .47; several judges achieved correlations in the vicinity of .70. Judges were thus able to make reasonable a priori assessments of the size of the effects produced by the treatments as briefly described to them.

A similar strategy was utilized to assess the ability of experts in personality and social psychology to estimate the strength of manipulations from studies taken from the *Journal of Personality and Social Psychology*. Manipulation checks are frequently used to test the "take" of independent variables, and the results of these checks provide a standard to

compare judgments of the strengths of treatment. When judges' estimates were averaged and the estimate for each manipulation was correlated with the actual manipulation check value, a correlation coeffi-
cient of .84 was obtained. Although these findings show only that judges can agree as to which treatments are likely to produce the largest
effects, we believe they bear indirectly on judges' ability to agree in estimating effect sizes, even when, as with the social psychology manipulation checks, not all the outcome measures are in the same metric. We
believe experts' judgments offer promise as a reasonable barometer of
the magnitude of experimental effects.

Precedent exists within the behaviorist framework for making a
posteriori judgment of the size of experimental effect demonstrated.
Visual rather than statistical analysis is used as the general standard for
acceptance into the *Journal of Applied Behavioral Analysis* (Michael, 1974).
Reviewers expert in the given problem area judge whether a solution to
a socially significant problem area has been demonstrated, paying particular attention to the graphic display in determining whether the
effect "looks big." As Baer (1977, p. 171) has said, "If a problem has
been solved, you can *see* that. . . . This, after all, was the major conclusion to be made, not whether an experimental effect had been uncov-
ered." Regrettably, the factors influencing these judgments of outcomes have only recently begun to be studied (see DeProspero, 1976;
Jones, Weinrott, and Vaught, 1978).

Normative Approaches. Evaluators are seldom in a position to
employ absolute standards for assessing the applied significance of outcome measures. Medical interventions that save lives or increase life
expectancy may represent instances where there is nearly universal
agreement regarding treatment value, "nearly" because there are
always the "what ifs?" What if the time and money spent on this intervention had been expended with an alternative treatment that saved
more lives or saved the same number of lives with younger, smarter,
healthier persons? What if the intervention extended the patient's life
expectancy six years but produced recurring nausea and dizziness
while an alternative treatment produced a three-year reprieve from
death with few side effects? Clearly, issues of quality should be raised,
as Ball has pointed out so forcefully in his contribution to this sourcebook.

More common is the case where some comparative standard is
employed to gauge the size of an experimental effect. A novel approach
to weight control is applauded when outcomes are larger than previous
modification efforts; a treatment to increase compliance with a medical

regimen is abandoned when results are smaller than existing treatments. A method of preventive dentistry is adopted if it is cheaper than other methods showing otherwise similar outcomes. Such comparative standards require data from other interventions with the same problem and outcome measure. It may be useful to know that a new approach to cigarette smoking control causes 50 percent of the participants to quit smoking if this quit rate is better than that achieved in most studies that attempt to induce participants to abstain from substance abuse if, and this is admittedly a big if, we can assume the problem areas are similarly resistant to change. It would be even more useful to know that this new approach to cigarette smoking control causes more participants to quit smoking than 90 percent of all other smoking modification methods. Policy decisions could be greatly simplified (but political, financial, and ethical considerations scarcely make them automatic) if this information were available.

Illustrations. An experiment by Jeffrey, Wing, and Stunkard (1976) utilized norms to assess the impact made in their efforts to bring about weight loss with obese participants. A mean weight loss of 11.5 pounds found in twenty-one previous studies compared favorably with the 11.0-pound average reported in their study. Should these methods of weight control be adopted by a community mental health clinic? Unless the treatment had secondary selling points (for example, delivered by paraprofessionals in large groups in sessions of limited duration), the magnitude of its effect is not particularly persuasive.

We have conducted a meta-analysis of forty-one recent smoking studies reporting percentage decrease in smoking. When the data from the experimental groups in these studies are averaged across all followup periods reported, the mean decrease in smoking was 53 percent, with a standard deviation of 27 percent. We might be inclined to call large those scores beyond one standard deviation from the mean, but such large standard deviations suggest marked disparity in the impacts of treatments as well as a nonnormal distribution. The standard deviation at the popular six-month follow-up point is still a rather substantial 22 percent. However, only 14 percent of the data points at six months were above 60 percent. We may be inclined to term a 70 percent decrease in smoking at the end of six months big simply because such decreases occur so infrequently. When the distribution of scores is not normal and cannot be legitimately abbreviated with a mean and standard deviation, a frequency distribution of the data offers a viable alternative as a standard to deduce large and small effect sizes.

Smith and Glass (1977) have utilized a similar technique to

aggregate the results of nearly four hundred psychotherapy and counseling studies. For their purposes, the authors defined effect size as the "mean difference between the treated and control subjects divided by the standard deviation of the control group" (p. 753). They reported a mean superiority of .68 standard deviations of experimental groups over control groups as their average effect size. Given an effect size standard deviation of .67 sigma, we would likely be no more than marginally impressed with a study demonstrating a .50 sigma experimental versus control group superiority. We might, on the other hand, be very enthusiastic about an innovative treatment showing an effect size beyond 2 sigmas.

The Smith and Glass meta-analysis illustrates a critical caution in effect size estimation studies. The point, also addressed in Ball's chapter in this volume, concerns the choice of comparison group or condition made by the researcher. It is foolish to imagine an experimenter would make decisions that would tend to diminish chances of producing a large experimental effect, should effect size become a new criterion to evaluate the worth of research. Therefore, a control group might be chosen solely to maximize the difference between experimental and control group scores. In the psychotherapy case, this might mean using a homogeneous control group (thus reducing the control group sigma in the denominator of the effect size indicator) that had never previously received psychotherapy (thus moving the control group mean in the numerator away from the experimental group mean). Campbell's (1975) notion of a corruptible indicator argues cogently for the very real possibility of this occurrence. Should our norms be periodically updated (as we maintain they should) by inclusion of this new psychotherapy study, it follows that the standard would become more stringent for the next researcher whose results are being compared to previous work in the field.

Quantity versus Quality of Change

Normative standards offer promise as a means of skirting otherwise subjective assessments of effect size magnitude. But subjective impressions of the change demonstrated in research may have greater clinical significance than the mere quantitative modifications made. For instance, a program that induces obese subjects to lose eleven pounds may not alter a subject's feelings of self-worth if no one else notices the change. A treatment to modify a husband's negative interactions with his wife may reduce the number of nagging statements to zero but go unnoticed by his spouse. We must distinguish carefully between qualitative and quantitative measures of change, a point made in another context by Ball (this volume), with which we would heartily concur. Said slightly differently, we must not be deluded into maintaining that we have produced large effects simply because the comparative size of the quantitative change is substantial.

Each study that reports the percentage decrease in hyperactive behavior of young children might also supply ratings of the extent to which parents and teachers notice the beneficial changes on rating scale assessments. Should a new intervention produce a three-point change (on a seven-point scale) in ratings by parents, we could reasonably term this a large effect, knowing that previous efforts had never produced more than a two-point change. Knowing that parents give more physical affection would further substantiate our claims for the importance of the change. If this study reduced the percentage of hyperactivity consistently below 5 percent, a change greater than 95 percent of previous studies, we should be further convinced this is a big effect, and we might strive for this quantitative standard as a goal in subsequent treatment programs prior to knowing the responses of parents and teachers.

The relationship between quantity and quality of change may often be inverse; small quantitative change may be associated with superior qualitative change while large quantitative change may be of inferior quality. The change in speech involved in dropping out racial slurs and implications of inferiority is a relatively small one, but the change in quality of interracial relations might be experienced as substantial. There have been reports on the coronary artery bypass operation that indicate the surgery does not prolong life but improves quality of life during the survival time (see Weinstein, Pliskin, and Stason, 1977). Presumably, also, there might be large quantitative changes of low quality. For example, a football coach might want some of his players to participate in a program to increase weight, but he would be dissatisfied if the increase were fat rather than muscle. A gain in reading ability reflected only in faster reading of comic books might not be regarded as much of an improvement.

Applied behavior analysts have always placed great stock in the quantitative assessment of behavior change but have only recently begun to recognize the importance of qualitative measures of change (see Wolf, 1978). This approach is termed *social validation*, to reflect directly the reliance upon pertinent members of society rather than the research audience as the appropriate group to substantiate presumed treatment benefits. For example, Fawcett and Miller (1975) asked judges to rate the public speaking ability of subjects before and after training. Clear differences in these pre–post ratings validated quantitative changes in public speaking; that is, the changes were sufficient to be discriminated by judges. However, a survey of several studies in the *Journal of Applied Behavior Analysis* (Yeaton, in press) suggests that rating scale changes are rather inelastic; large, absolute changes in the dependent variable are associated with small, absolute changes (less than three points) on a seven-point, semantic differential scale. Specification of other dependent variables may yield slightly smaller quantitative change but decidedly larger qualitative change. These results tend empirically to substantiate our caution that apparently large effects may be a wishful delusion.

We do not, unfortunately, know much about assessing quality of change, let alone know how to factor it into our judgments about the worth of interventions. Probably most persons assume there is a linear, and certainly monotonic, relationship between quantity and quality of change. Thus, for example, it is tempting to suppose improvement in reading ability is to be valued. But if, as seems likely, various kinds of reading materials are prepared deliberately for particular levels of reading ability, a modest change between levels might make little difference at all. For example, if most reading materials are programmed at, say, the fourth-grade level (comics) or the eighth-grade level (newspapers), improvement in reading ability from fourth- to fifth-grade level might actually make few new reading experiences available. For many variables, the relationship between quantity and quality of change will most likely not be linear and perhaps not even be invariably monotonic. The relationship between years of education and various indicators of quality of life may well be nonlinear, probably characterized by plateaus and step-wise changes. There may be very little advantage to having completed eleven years of school as opposed to ten but a large advantage to having completed twelve years of school as opposed to eleven. Similarly, the advantage of being able to read at the fifth-grade rather than the fourth-grade level may be negligible (even though that would be a 25 percent improvement) because no other changes flow from that one.

At present, we can do little more than urge investigators to consider carefully the quality of the changes they are investigating and to attempt to use their quality estimates to form their judgments about the importance of the quantitative changes they are able to demonstrate.

Dependent Variable Scaling Problems

Effect size may be difficult to determine accurately because the units in which the dependent variable is scaled may not be equal at all points on the scale. For example, Jencks (Yankelovich, 1979) has produced evidence on amount of education that suggests there are discontinuities in the meaning of increasing amounts of education. Thus, for black males, there is no advantage in completing high school if they are not going on to college. There may be little advantage in going on to college if they are not going to complete the bachelor's degree. Such findings suggest programs that produce increments in amount of education, for example, by keeping youth in school, have to be evaluated with great care lest seemingly large effects, for example, an additional year and a half of education, be the basis for policies ineffective in the long run. It is probable that inequalities in the units in which dependent variables are scaled are the rule rather than the exception.

One particular source of inequality is likely to be the point on the scale characterizing a target person or group, in that it will almost certainly not be equally easy to produce change at all points on the scale. It will, for example, certainly be easier to take a group of teenage males who run a hundred yards in 12 seconds and improve their running speed by .5 seconds than to take a group who run a hundred yards in 10 seconds and improve their speed by the same amount. Generally speaking, it will be easier to produce improvement in groups functioning below the population mean than to produce the same improvement in those functioning above the mean. Consequently, what would be a rather small gain for one group might be a large one for another, as assessed by the effort required to produce it.

Strength and Integrity. The development of a set of techniques to estimate the magnitude of an effect presupposes certain considerations of the strength and integrity of the treatment involved. Sechrest and colleagues (Sechrest and Redner, forthcoming; Sechrest and others, 1979) have elaborated upon strength and integrity issues in the context of research in criminal justice and evaluation, although our discussion must, of necessity, be much briefer. Strength refers to the a priori, planned intensity of treatment delivery. For example, therapy might be administered in a strong form by utilizing therapists in a one-to-one manner. Integrity of treatment, the degree to which the plan of delivery is implemented, can be ascertained only by careful monitoring and is free to vary independent of treatment strength. Since magnitudes of effects depend integrally upon both the strength and integrity of treatments, any assessment of intervention impact is open to question without knowledge of both strength and integrity.

Outcome measures expressed as norms offer a means for validating judged treatment strengths. We would be embarrassed if a strong treatment produced an effect estimated to be two standard deviations *below* the mean of other experimental groups treated for the same problem. Consistency of a priori judgments of treatment strength and a posteriori normative standards form a basis for ranking treatments classified along theoretical and process dimensions. For example, it is plausible to expect prompting procedures for fingernail biting to produce smaller habit decrements than, say, self-monitoring procedures, which may in turn be inferior to financial reinforcement contingencies. It would be insightful to discover the same ordinal relationship among these three treatments regardless of the problem domain. We would then be in the privileged position of recommending a treatment proportional to the judged severity of the presenting problem. Very strong treatments would not be recommended for mild problems. We are likely to apply a "weakest that works" principle both to preserve valuable resources and to avoid general client adaptation to strong doses of treatments.

Small immediate treatment effects might grow over time (Gilbert, Light, and Mosteller, 1975); an initial "nudge" might set a person off on a course that would produce large ultimate change just as a small force will set a ski jumper into motion. Indeed, many tested treatments seem implicitly to bank on the nudge notion, since they are, on the face of it, sufficiently weak as to make it scarcely imaginable that any profound change would be found immediately. Thus, for example, the group counseling program Kassebaum, Ward, and Wilner (1971) tested as an antidote to criminal recidivism involved only an hour or two of counseling per week by often not very well-trained counselors and often in large groups. However, the program was expected to reduce commitment to criminal life-styles and ultimately to reduce criminal behavior.

London (1977) has written about the twin but opposite processes of cumulative convergence and cumulative divergence. *Cumulative convergence* refers to any process that, once set in motion, tends to produce convergence toward some "normal" state. *Cumulative divergence* is an opposite process that tends to produce greater and greater divergence from normal. No matter how unusual the initial distribution of a set of numbers, integers, let us say, ranging from one to nine, additional randomly generated numbers will tend to produce a convergence of the distribution toward equal appearance of the nine integers. Similarly, the learning of speech is a cumulatively convergent process, since infants gradually come to sound more and more like the persons around them. An initial error in the trajectory of a missile, however, is a cumulatively divergent process, since the farther the missile travels, the farther off target it will be. In criminology, labeling theory describes a cumulatively divergent process in which the initially small act of identifying a youth as a delinquent is assumed to initiate a process that will produce greater and greater social deviation.

The implication of this discussion is that seemingly small treatment effects might really be large in their long-run implications, and, therefore, when nudges are achieved, they should be causes for elation (or despair if the change is in the wrong direction). The problem as we see it is that we do not often have a very good way of deciding when we have achieved a genuine nudge as opposed to a genuine small effect; the distinction is important. The optimism surrounding early Head Start programs, especially when it seemed there were some favorable outcomes, was based on the notion that a cumulatively convergent process that would cause experientially deprived children to become gradually more and more like their more favored classmates had been set in motion. In retrospect, the effects, such as they were, were less like nudges than just simply small, transient effects.

We do not know how to determine whether an effect is small but likely to grow as opposed to being simply small. Perhaps a careful study of effects that have proved to be of the nudge type would be informative and a basis for developing some expectations about cumulative processes. Assuming labeling theory to be correct, why does identifying a youngster as a delinquent have such profound effects, while labeling another as a bloomer (see the Pygmalion effect, Rosenthal and Jacobson, 1968) have a much more elusive and transient effect (see Lindgren, 1976)? We need to know.

Aggregation of Small Effects

There may be outcomes of interventions that, although small in a specific instance, may nonetheless be large when aggregated across a large number of units. For example, the improvement in gas mileage from reducing driving speed to fifty-five miles per hour might not be enough to effect savings that would be meaningful to most individual drivers, but the aggregated saving of gasoline would have a very important impact on this nation's oil consumption. Or relatively small changes in average sentence length for certain classes of criminal offenders would have large effects on the number of incarcerated persons in our jails and prisons at any one time. Charitable organizations such as the March of Dimes have successfully raised substantial sums of money by a plea to each individual to contribute only extra small change.

But not all small effects would necessarily become important even if aggregated, because at least some effects have implications only at the individual level. A small increase in reading ability, even if aggregated across large numbers of persons, would still remain a small increase in reading ability. Or if a nutritional rehabilitation program produced an average height increase of one centimeter in nutritionally deprived children (see McKay and others, 1978), those children would remain short, and the aggregated effects would be nil. We once encountered a newspaper article that referred to an estimate of the nationally aggregated loss in IQ points supposedly attributable to smoking. Somehow or other, the idea of a nation "losing" millions of IQ points does not seem to get at the nature of the problem.

However, even small effects at the mean could be large at the extremes if the effect were uniform across the entire distribution of values. Imagine, for example, a population of one million children with a mean IQ of 85 and assume a standard deviation in the IQ measure of fifteen. Assume also that an IQ of 125 is required as a minimum for successful completion of a premedical education. In that population, there would be only about 3,900 persons bright enough to complete a premedical education. Suppose, then, a compensatory education program were devised that would raise the mean IQ by five points and have a uniform effect throughout the distribution. There would then be more than 9,000 children bright enough to complete premedical education, a more than twofold increase. The effect of the program would have very limited implications at the mean of the population, but the practical implications at the extreme upper end would surely be accounted quite important.

Effects may also be aggregated across time at the individual level. If people are constrained from smoking by laws or customs limiting smoking in many places, and if they do not compensate by smoking when it is permissible, the aggregate effect across a lifetime could amount to many, many cigarettes. A reduction of food intake by one hundred calories per day would produce a weight loss of about ten pounds over the course of one year. The daily change in weight, or even the weekly change, would be undetectable, but the effect accumulated over time would be sizable.

Treatment Costs and Benefits

Had we the capacity to manufacture an inexpensive yet harmless pill that could cure cancer, we might term the magnitude of the effect, at the very least, gargantuan. More realistically, we would applaud a novel treatment for anorexia nervosa that produced greater benefits than standard treatments at the same cost or the same benefits at smaller costs. The cost-benefit basis for decision making is seldom so simple as this sketch implies, as Levine has articulated so cogently in this sourcebook. What dollar value would one place on the benefit of an overweight person losing forty pounds? It is difficult even to list all the benefits, let alone place a dollar value on them. What about the cost of a new wardrobe and a new diet and a divorce? A divorce? Perhaps! Neill, Marshall, and Yale (1978) report a retrospective interview study of the adverse material changes experienced by fourteen patients who underwent intestinal bypass surgery. Unintended side effects are at least as difficult to place a dollar value on as to predict.

Why should we bother to assess the effectiveness of research? At a fundamental level, we probably wish to demonstrate our understanding of the phenomenon or problem under study. An effectiveness measure may be a particularly convincing bit of evidence in making the case to the reader that we have located and perhaps controlled the most important variables associated with the phenomenon in question. Very often we wish to infer that a practical solution to a problem has been discovered. Such an inference is particularly plausible, should a large effect size be shown using either a judgmental or a normative approach. Furthermore, we assume staff and administrative personnel are more likely to initiate and maintain procedures that exhibit large rather than small magnitudes of effect. But even our preliminary efforts to articulate the conceptual issues that bear on the effectiveness assessment problem suggest the problem is not inclined to yield to a solution without relentless and sophisticated scrutiny. Even the most *potentially* convincing demonstration of our understanding of the functional relationship among critical variables and a hint of the discovery of an eminently practical solution to the problem may not be perceived to be of meaningful magnitude by the audience of relevance (see Sechrest and Yeaton, 1979a). This may be a simple matter of presentation of data and rhetoric of results, or a more basic deficiency in the public understanding of the logic of scientific questioning and answering. Our quest is then not so different from that of the artist who strives to produce a technically perfect work that expresses a beauty visible to all its beholders.

References

Baer, D. M. "Perhaps It Would Be Better Not to Know Everything." *Journal of Applied Behavior Analysis,* 1977, *10* (1), 167–172.

Campbell, D. T. "Assessing the Impact of Planned Social Change." In G. M. Lyons (Ed.), *Social Research and Public Policies: The Dartmouth/OECD Conference.* Hanover, N.H.: Public Affairs Center, Dartmouth College, 1975.

DeProspero, A. "A Comparison of Visual and Statistical Analyses of Intrasubject Replication Data." Paper presented at the meeting of the Association for the Advancement of Behavior Therapy, New York, 1976.

Fawcett, S. B., and Miller, L. K. "Training Public-Speaking Behavior: An Experimental Analysis and Social Validation." *Journal of Applied Behavioral Analysis,* 1975, *8* (2), 125–135.

Gilbert, J. P., Light, R. J., and Mosteller, F. "Assessing Social Interventions: An Empirical Basis for Policy." In C. A. Bennett and A. A. Lumsdaine (Eds.), *Evaluation and Experiment: Some Critical Issues in Assessing Social Programs.* New York: Academic Press, 1975.

Jeffrey, R. W., Wing, R. R., and Stunkard, A. J. "Behavioral Treatment of Obesity: The State of the Art 1976." *Behavior Therapy,* 1976, *9* (2), 189–199.

Jones, R. R., Weinrott, M. R., and Vaught, R. S. "Effects of Serial Dependency on the Agreement Between Visual and Statistical Inference." *Journal of Applied Behavioral Analysis,* 1978, *11* (2), 277–283.

Kassebaum, G., Ward, D. A., and Wilner, D. M. *Prison Treatment and Parole Survival.* New York: Wiley, 1971.

Lindgren, H. C. *Educational Psychology in the Classroom.* (5th ed.) New York: Wiley, 1976.

London, I. D. "Convergent and Divergent Amplification and Its Meaning for Social Science." *Psychological Reports,* 1977, *41,* 111–123.

McKay, H., and others. "Improving Cognitive Ability in Chronically Deprived Children." *Science,* 1978, *200,* 270–278.

McSweeny, A. J. "Effects of Response Cost on the Behavior of a Million Persons: Charging for Directory Assistance in Cincinnati." *Journal of Applied Behavior Analysis,* 1978, *11* (1), 47–51.

Michael, J. "Statistical Inference for Individual Organism Research: Mixed Blessing or Curse?" *Journal of Applied Behavior Analysis,* 1974, *7* (4), 647–653.

Neill, J. R., Marshall, J. R., and Yale, C. E. "Marital Changes After Intestinal Bypass Surgery." *Journal of the American Medical Association,* 1978, *240* 447–450.

Rosenthal, R., and Jacobson, L. *Pygmalion in the Classroom: Teacher Expectation and Pupils' Intellectual Development.* New York: Holt, Rinehart and Winston, 1968.

Sechrest, L., and Redner, R. *Strength and Integrity of Treatments in Evaluation Studies,* forthcoming.

Sechrest, L., West, S. C., Phillips, M. A., Redner, R., and Yeaton, W. "Some Neglected Problems in Evaluation Research: Strength and Integrity of Treatments." In L. Sechrest and others (Eds.), *Evaluation Studies Review Annual,* Vol. 4. Beverly Hills, Calif.: Sage, 1979.

Sechrest, L., and Yeaton, W. E. *Empirical Approaches to Effect Size Estimation.* Unpublished manuscript, Florida State University, 1979a.

Sechrest, L., and Yeaton, W. E. "Estimating Magnitudes of Experimental Effects." Unpublished manuscript, 1979b.

Smith, M. L., and Glass, G. V. "Meta-Analysis of Psychotherapy Outcome Studies." *American Psychologist,* 1977, *32,* 752–760.

Weinstein, M. C., Pliskin, J. S., and Stason, W. B. "Coronary Artery Bypass Surgery: Decision and Policy Analysis." In J. P. Bunker, B. A. Barnes, and F. Mosteller (Eds.), *Costs, Risks, and Benefits of Surgery.* New York: Oxford University Press, 1977.

56

Wolf, M. M. "Social Validity: The Case for Subjective Measurement or How Applied Behavioral Analysis Is Finding Its Heart." *Journal of Applied Behavior Analysis,* 1978, *11* (2), 203–214.

Yankelovich, D. "Who Gets Ahead in America." *Psychology Today,* July 1979, *13* (2), 28–91.

Yeaton, W. E., "A Critique of the Effectiveness Dimension in Applied Behavior Analysis." *Journal of Applied Behavior Analysis,* in press.

Lee Sechrest is professor of psychology at Florida State University,
where he teaches courses in research methodology and program
evaluation. Previously he was at Northwestern University,
where he was involved in the development of their
training program in evaluation research. Sechrest is
a consultant to a number of government and private
agencies involved in development and evaluation
of social interactions.

William E. Yeaton received his Ph.D. in psychology in 1979 from
Florida State University. He served as an assistant editor for the
fourth volume of the Evaluation Studies Review Annual
(1979). His research interests include program
evaluation, empirical validation of procedures for
diffusion of effective treatments, and behavioral
community psychology.

*Considerable care must be taken to define those groups or individuals
most concerned with program impact. The consumer of a service
is clearly of primary importance. It is possible to increase
program effectiveness for the consumer through the use
of certain guiding principles based on the extension
of existing quality assurance and program
evaluation methodologies.*

Service Delivery and Evaluation from the Consumer's Point of View

Thomas J. Kiresuk
Sander H. Lund
Susan K. Schultz

The recipient of a service is only one element in an array of constituencies that influence the operation of a service program. Other elements in this context include funding sources, national and local legislative and governing bodies, professional standards and groups, the human services knowledge network, the program's table of organization, and the community at large. All service programs operate in such a context, but for any particular program at any time, the importance of any element can vary greatly. Conceptually, the elements represent terms in a regression equation or multidimensional vector analysis, with each making an individual contribution to the direction of program development. There is some residual variation that can be attributed to the particular style and philosophy of the program, but all these forces must strike some sort of balance. Program capacity to be responsive to this context, to adapt to it, to influence it, and to be knowledgeable and capable in the process of change determine the ultimate likelihood of its survival and success.

Several of the elements in the context mentioned could be considered consumers or consumer representatives. The taxpayers and their representatives, for example, are consumers in the sense that they purchase public services. More typically, however, the consumer is thought of as a user, or potential user, of a service. Consumer representatives in the form of community organizations or board members, and legally deputized or informally self-selected client representatives, comprise other segments in the consumer block. It is in the sense of consumer as recipient of services that we use the term in this chapter.

Ideally, in order to enhance program growth and development, all the constituencies in the context of relevance should have an avenue of meaningful input into the program's operation. This does not mean the organization should surrender all its control mechanisms to outside forces or that it can or should attempt to meet all the demands of all its constituencies all the time. What is required, rather, is an accountability mechanism that helps identify and address legitimate external concerns but does not sacrifice a program's need for responsible direction of its own destiny and development. Accordingly, the consumer point of view translates into finding ways to use existing power within the context of relevance to improve the relative balance of power in favor of the consumer without destroying the present system or compromising its current level of effectiveness. This approach to sociopolitical change is incremental; our intention is to improve the present system by reshaping it through corrective feedback from its context of relevance rather than destroying it and starting anew.

The Proposed Model

The accountability model proposed here takes the form of an integrated, goal-oriented program evaluation and quality assurance mechanism. Such a mechanism would have three dynamic components: (1) development of a program goal structure based on iterative surveys of program constituencies, (2) formulation of service goals through client input, and (3) auditing of service goals by special-interest groups to identify and mitigate potential sources of bias. Although the complete model has not yet been fully tested, its various elements have emerged from the experience of diverse human services programs and promise to provide a basis for enhancing program effectiveness by shaping its operation according to feedback from its context of relevance. We describe each component of the proposed model.

Program Goal Structure. The basic structure for the proposed model is provided by Management by Objectives (MBO), which, as the name implies, is a means to administer an organization through the formulation and follow-up of specific, time-limited goals and objectives (Drucker, 1964). The essential characteristic of MBO is development of a hierarchical program goal structure. At the peak of such a structure is a statement of the program's ultimate mission; subordinate to the mission are concrete objectives that lead to the mission; subordinate to the objectives are specific goals. Objectives and goals are typically derived through negotiation with concerned program staff and are modified on the basis of past goal attainment.

Relevant to the construction of an integrated accountability structure, a modified version of MBO has been reported by Spano and Lund (1976) and elaborated by Spano, Kiresuk, and Lund (1977). In this system, the usual MBO format is supplemented by a statement of program philosophy and by shaping the program goal structure according to periodic surveys of a program's various constituencies. The program mission is superseded by a statement of program philosophy. Derived from literature reviews, community meetings, hospital policies, and staff discussions, the philosophy is a statement of a program's overall dedication, serving as background for examination and revision of the goal structure. The philosophy attempts to give continuity and subjective meaning to a program's operation by providing a sense of its fundamental but previously unarticulated value system. Such a statement can mitigate potential turmoil by assuring that a program's values are subject to scrutiny by its various audiences, thus providing a channel for incorporating legitimate external input into the program's operation.

The second novel component of the MBO format Spano and Lund advocate is periodic surveying of groups and individuals with a continuing interest or investment in a program's development. Sources of input for such surveys could include clients, legislators, community agencies, or professional organizations. A panel of individuals representing each group is contacted annually to get input on future priorities and feedback on the degree to which past priorities were satisfied. The results of such surveys are employed to make appropriate modifications in the program's goal structure.

Client Input in Treatment Goals. Although the capstone of meaningful evaluation in the human services seems to be determination of client outcome, disagreement regarding the nature of a "good" outcome often makes this form of assessment problematic. Davis (1973) has described the development of a new form of outcome evaluation called Individualized Goal Attainment (IGA) measurement, wherein generalized effectiveness standards are supplanted by criteria tailored to the needs, aspirations, and capabilities of the individual recipient. A prominent form of IGA measurement is Goal Attainment Scaling, in which client-specific goals (determined during the intake session) are scaled according to a five-point range of potential outcomes — from "most unfavorable treatment outcome thought likely" to "best antici- pated success with treatment" (see Kiresuk and Sherman, 1968). At fol- low-up, each scale is scored to determine attainment level.

Although originally intended as a means for clinicians to set treatment goals, IGA measurement devices were quickly adapted to permit client involvement in goal setting. Lombillo, Kiresuk, and Sherman (1973), for example, have described a variant of Goal Attain- ment Scaling called Contract Fulfillment Analysis wherein treatment goals are negotiated between client and clinician; Jones and Garwick (1973) report on Guide to Goals, a programmed form of Goal Attain- ment Scaling where goal setting is left completely up to service recipi- ents.

By serving as a vehicle for active client involvement in the treat- ment process, IGA measurement devices not only apply evaluation cri- teria but also have the potential to (1) enhance negotiation of mutually agreed treatment contracts, (2) monitor the problems and expectations typical of clients seeking services at a program, (3) facilitate problem clarification, and (4) enhance client treatment motivation. Relevant to this last point, there is substantial evidence that client participation in treatment goal setting has a positive effect on clinical outcomes (Calsyn and LaFerriere, in press; Galano, 1977; Houts and Scott, 1975; Jones and Garwick, 1973; Smith, 1976). Although the dynamic of the goal- setting effect is not yet clear, involvement in goal setting may free the client from a passive role and encourage active commitment to the treatment process. Client involvement in goal setting is a basic means to amend the power discrepancy between client and clinician and to help assure that the services a program supplies are in some sense appropriate to the self-identified needs of its basic constituency.

Goal Setting as a Quality Assurance Method. The use of goal- oriented treatment, record keeping, and evaluation procedures also allows auditing of goals to assess the quality and appropriateness of the services provided to specific populations. A procedure such as Goal

Attainment Scaling, for example, records treatment purposes, provides an index of individual progress, and offers evidence of therapeutic intent and outcome. This kind of information is essential to answering accountability questions.

There is a variety of ways to use IGA devices to determine program accountability to specific service groups and subgroups. For example, using the Goal Attainment Score as an outcome measure, the efficacy of diverse therapies can be determined for different ethnic groups or diagnostic categories. If a particular form of therapy were found to be differentially more effective for a particular group, it would then be possible to direct members of that group to the preferred form of treatment. A variant of this procedure would be to use Goal Attainment Scaling to determine which types of treatment are more or less successful in dealing with specific problem areas or goal categories.

Although the Goal Attainment Follow-up Guide is often intended for use in evaluating service outcomes, it is also part of a client's treatment record and as such may be used in concurrent and retrospective reviews of care. Follow-up guides could be used in auditing for special concerns of specific populations. For example, an increasingly articulated special concern of women using mental health services is the potential for sex-role stereotyping by clinicians and consequent sexist bias in treatment. The follow-up guide for a particular woman could be reviewed for evidence of sexist treatment bias. If the content of treatment goals seems to reflect such bias, further inquiry into the nature of services provided would be warranted. As an additional safeguard against inappropriate treatment, such audits might even be conducted with the participation of representatives of the group involved. A concurrent audit using Goal Attainment Scaling might be usefully incorporated into a clinical case conference. This would allow peer review of follow-up guide quality, which quickly becomes routine, and peer interaction around more difficult issues, such as bias. At the program level, review of follow-up guides could involve aggregation of goal content and Goal Attainment Scores for particular subgroups of clients to derive profiles and care patterns. These might help identify bias or ineffectiveness in particular aspects of a program's service provision.

Guiding Principles

Increasing the effectiveness of the existing service delivery system does not require radical restructuring from without but rather decentralization of information gathering so all legitimate participants in the human services enterprise have the opportunity to express and protect their interests. One means to accomplish this is the utilization and extension of existing quality assurance and program evaluation methodologies, such as the integrated model proposed here. In making this extension, however, one must keep in mind several guiding principles. These principles are part of conventional wisdom in the human services delivery systems; they are cautionary notes frequently expressed by administrators, providers, and consumers.

First, *save the consumer from the worst abuses of the service delivery system.* There should be some way to prevent intentional or unintentional exploitation. Monetary and personal exploitation are monitored through various ethics committees and appeal structures in the traditional professions and services but may not be in newer or proposed services.

Second, *help the system be responsive to its own codes of ethics and practice.* While related to the first principle, this concept moves the emphasis from a nondisruptive, discreet, self-policing stance of the service provider toward more formal, routinized scanning of the system to ensure compliance. The "patient rights" monitoring of systems such as those in the Michigan public mental health system is an example of this.

Third, *ensure safety.* Potential negative side effects of treatment should be monitored, reacted to when indicated, and the client made aware of these risks. While this is a topic of debate, especially with regard to the appropriate extent of awareness and manner of informing the client, new and proposed treatments may lack the research and development that would document these risks, and advocates of the treatment may be slow to discuss them.

Fourth, *ensure quality.* While a quality control system may be good for averting disaster, it may not be good at preventing simple backsliding. The treatment demonstrated in the laboratory may not be the treatment the consumer receives. There should be some way of relating the two standards of practice. In addition, one would expect variation in treatment quality. The quality control system should detect unusual deviation and slow drifts away from usual performance standards.

Fifth, *be of reasonable cost to client, profession, and government.* From the consumer point of view, complex, time-consuming, expensive evaluation and quality control is not an advantage. All that is required are simple, straightforward, perhaps inelegant methods that meet the needs listed here. The system has to meet the needs of an array of constituencies, of course, but from this point of view, the direct and self-evident system is the best one.

Sixth, *help guide the service industry.* The test of an evaluation system to see if it is really only a required but unutilized program appendage would be the consumer's questions "Does anybody use all of this stuff?" and "Does it really make any difference how it all turns out?" For instance, indicators of treatment outcome and consumer satisfaction may be linked not at all to program mission, objectives, and goals.

Seventh, *be flexible enough to meet changing and multiple needs.* Evaluation conducted according to standards for quality control established during a previous era may indicate apparently stabile or high achievement yet may not be relevant to current consumers.

Eighth, *be responsive to a range of populations.* Professional and social-political-religious ideologies may be inherent in a particular treatment. Are these compatible with the clients' needs or are they an enforced characteristic that must be adopted in order to receive treatment? Is this part of the transaction open and above board? Does the evaluation system pick up mismatches or reflect ideological characteristics?

Ninth, *be responsive to ambiance and atmosphere,* the less tangible aspects of service delivery. The opinion of the service provider is not enough here. Contrary to what one might expect, consumers may not mind a crowded waiting room, which some may find revealing and supportive. But the consumers might very well mind the fact that the visible coffee was available to staff and not clients, that some eligibility workers might provide moral lectures to some clients, and that some therapists might drift off to sleep (and snore). These are not the kinds of things existing processes and outcome measures would be likely to include.

Tenth, *make the consumers informed about their choices.* While cumbersome to the provider and, if done inappropriately, to the consumer, the system should document the presence of informed consent regarding traditional experimentation, treatments provided as sound when they really may be untested, and the willingness to participate in socio-political movements — the use of patients to disrupt elements of the existing system in order to bring about change.

Eleventh, *help make the consumers active participants in their own treatment.* While this is an ideological stance that may not be appropriate or desired by all consumers, the system should document the provision of the opportunity to take part in treatment.

And twelfth, *make the service delivery responsive to the consumers' capacity to adopt the treatments.* The compliance literature suggests the client's readiness to adopt treatment is a major factor in its follow-through and success. Assuming it is all a matter of psychoanalytic transference is no longer enough.

The counterpoint to these twelve characteristics of evaluation and quality control systems are the following characteristics they should not have. The system should not be burdensome, interfering, or inhibiting to the service industry to the extent that it becomes destructive. The consumer will not be aided by a system that requires too many forms to be filled out or that has a staff who feel cornered, stepped on, or mistreated.

The system should not prevent program growth or change for the better. If the measures are chosen and used in a way to ensure compliance with present program directives only, the capacity to revise the program and incorporate new methods will be inhibited. Consumers would be cut off from potential program improvement by the very devices designed to protect them.

The system should not add unreasonably or prohibitively to costs. It is possible that evaluative maintenance can constitute up to 80 percent of the total treatment costs. While the information may be of great value for research purposes and may contribute to the welfare of future clients, from the consumer point of view, this may be more evaluation than one needs or can use.

Last, the system should not be implemented in such a way that the total impact on the organization and service delivery is destructive. Judicious use of knowledge transfer methods and concepts might prevent program disruption resulting from naive or simpleminded implementation methods. Long- and short-term compliance with administrative and research directives can be considered comparable to innovations in the fields of education, agriculture, and individual patient care. Consumers may find it surprising that they ought to be concerned about how program changes on their behalf are implemented. However, staff morale, effectiveness and efficiency, the human and financial costs of the installation, and maintenance of program changes all bear on the nature of the services they receive.

The preceding may read like an arbitrarily devised catechism, but it is intended to provide a general framework of thinking and premises to which specific recommendations can be related. The following paragraphs spell out recommendations that would apply to the service delivery, program management, professional, and public policy levels.

Several authors have explored tangible methods of addressing these issues on the service delivery level. Baxter and Beaulieu (1974) worked out an elaborate process and outcome evaluation scheme that deals directly in an outpatient mental health setting with many of the consumer issues described earlier. These authors have not received adequate recognition for their achievement. The general themes guiding their system are clearly announced and, most important, they are converted into measures that would indicate how well these program directions are being carried out. Every statement and measure was meticulously tested for logical and procedural loopholes. Although the emerging system appeared deceptively self-evident, it provided reassurance that consumer concerns were receiving more than lip service; they were the subject of tangible and regularly used measures. The system we designed includes an evaluation scheme, effectiveness and efficiency objectives, and a therapist follow-up guide critique schedule. The evaluation scheme yields an index score for direct clinical services, which is derived from original and modified Goal Attainment Scale scores. Effectiveness and efficiency objectives follow from the goal statement for direct clinical services, which ensures that "an optimum volume of identified patients are efficiently provided with appropriate, acceptable referral, diagnostic, and treatment services that assist them in achieving patient-relevant, quality goals and with which they are reasonably satisfied" (Baxter and Beaulieu, 1974). Their Therapist Follow-up Guide Critique Schedule directly relates to the effectiveness and efficiency objectives, since it provides for systematic assessment of the psychotherapy goals established for each client.

For a related system in a crisis intervention center, Stelmachers, Lund, and Meade (1972) developed both client and program measures that would be responsive to consumer needs. In both the Baxter and Beaulieu and the Stelmachers examples, the system design and measures are "there for the taking." There is no reason for providers to postpone action in this area or to develop systems anew, at least from the consumer's point of view. The development and testing expense has already been invested, and special adaptations or elaborations could be easily accomplished and would probably serve the needs of most consumers.

Both these examples were developed to make evaluation relevant to program management. A highly developed system from the management point of view is that reported by Spano, Kiresuk, and Lund (1977), referred to earlier in the discussion of program goal structure. Starting with an explicitly described administrative context and working on through an array of program requirements (for example, Medicare-Medicaid mandates), the activity and outcome points of measurement have been intimately tied to the nature and purpose of our program. As with the previous system examples, the details of this system have been worked out — it is computerized, inexpensive (approximately $200 per year for keypunching and printouts), and probably more than the typical consumer would need. Points of access for the consumer in the form of audit and review are also available. Kiresuk and Schultz (1978) discuss accountability audits from the point of view of special populations of consumers, such as women and racial minorities.

With all the systems described, there is a considerable amount and variety of information available to program managers and others in the program's context of relevance. Experience with these systems so far suggests they may generate a little more information than most managers and administrators need or can utilize. The point here, however, is that these systems at least demonstrate ways to achieve responsiveness to consumers.

Experience in applying knowledge transfer concepts to the installation of evaluation into human services programs has been described by such authors as Fairweather, Sanders, and Tornatsky (1974) and, using another approach, Roy and Kiresuk (1977), Studer (1978), and Kiresuk and others (1977). This enterprise of applying knowledge transfer concepts is relatively new in terms of standards of scientific knowledge development but appears to have the kind of intuitively correct, commonsense attributes that would serve consumers' needs. Certainly, the idea that organizational resistance to planned change should be recognized and dealt with in advance of implementing evaluation is a central concern of this enterprise. In addition, a client's multifaceted reluctance or enthusiasm for treatment is a factor to be reckoned with in consumer-oriented service delivery. Here again, the methods based on concepts of knowledge transfer and planned change are available and, although in early form, are usable.

In terms of policy issues, there are some obvious recommendations. The research and development stage of novel human services treatments should be more extensive and have a consumer-oriented component. Routine consideration of a treatment should answer or address such questions as what is it, who is it for, with what expectations (including negative side effects), and at what cost. This is not to cast the pall of anti-intellectualism on the field of treatment research. This field is a vast, intricate, complex enterprise having many participants and constituencies. From the consumer's point of view, however, simply worded progress reports—including areas in which the answers are unknown—would be sufficient.

On the policy level, the distinction stressed by Klerman (1978) should be put forward—that therapy research is different from the study of therapy practice. While the former is of greater interest to scholars and researchers, the latter is crucial to consumers. The latter would stress fidelity of the practice to the entity researched in the laboratory, the amended list of side effects, and the actual varieties used in the field. There should be mandated evaluation and quality control of such possibilities as getting bad advice on telephone services, being exploited by volunteers, and being victimized by well-intentioned service providers. To guard against such violations in the future, perhaps a formally appointed board of consumer accreditation could be added to the array of accrediting organizations that currently exist in the national context of relevance surrounding service programs.

With regard to policy-level recommendations on the characteristics of evaluation and quality control systems, there already appears to be a steady march of events toward greater clarity and higher quality (*Evaluation and Change*, 1977). The inclusion of knowledge transfer concepts into this area would make the recommendations more realistic, feasible, and likely to be implemented and maintained.

Another policy area that could benefit from the inclusion of the consumer perspective is that of policies relating to alteration or innovation within the human services delivery system. Consumer impact studies could be routinely included in such large-scale changes as services integration and deinstitutionalization. Current practice appears to be to implement the change and then commission studies to see what happened. Knowledge transfer analyses and other forms of impact estimation — including small-scale pretesting — would help anticipate resistances and unanticipated side effects regarding both the community and the consumers.

Finally, at least for publicly funded service programs, some form of consumer-oriented communication devices should be required. There are several models that might be used, each of which has fixed headings applied across a variety of treatments or measurement devices. Among these models are the *Physician's Desk Reference,* Buros's *Mental Measurement Yearbooks,* and, probably most appropriate, information and referral manuals.

A recent format employed by a community information and referral service in describing a full range of services available in a major metropolitan area uses the following entries: Name or Organization, Address, For Information Call, Eligibility, Fees, Supported by, Hours, and Services Provided. Additional entries could include a fuller description of the nature of the service or treatment offered, its efficacy for various populations, its limitations and side effects, the nature of the personnel, and the presence or absence of certain features of evaluation and quality control, such as outcome measurement, follow-up, consumer satisfaction, and audit and utilization checks. Zusman and Slawson's (1972) Service Quality Profile suggests that ratings on related dimensions are possible. These ratings include administrative structure and procedures, staff training and qualification, staff commitment and morale, physical environment, patient integrity and safety, appropriateness of treatment, patient satisfaction, short-term outcome, and relative cost. Key references also could be listed. A human services yearbook that would summarize in detail the description, available information, pro and con discussion, and summary impression of all previously existing and novel treatments would be particularly useful. The intended audience for this yearbook would be the various classes of consumers described earlier. It could be written in a style that would appeal to service recipients as well as policy makers and administrators, and it could serve as a backup reference for the typical information and referral booklet. In this form, convenient, to-the-point information would be available to all classes of consumers.

If this chapter is to be true to its thesis, all the foregoing should be of some *demonstrable* benefit to the consumer. While efficacy research regarding these enterprises would be intriguing to the researcher, the consumer might rely on common sense and intuitive correctness of fit. It makes sense that a program that knows what it is trying to do, receives regular feedback on how well it is doing, and has routine reminders regarding its current and past consumers will be a better program. Research efforts comparable in magnitude to plumbing the major mysteries of nature would probably be seen as inappropriate.

There is some related research, however, that would support the concept that the recommendations listed here might prove beneficial. As noted earlier, client use of an evalution device, Guide to Goals, appears to have treatment facilitation effects in a variety of settings — mental health, family counseling, and rape counseling. It seems possible that client-oriented evaluation approaches will have similar facilitative effects in other settings. Studer's study of the organizational readiness for program evaluation measure included informal comments by program users indicating the existence of positive side effects from test taking and receiving the results of this measure. Stelmachers, Lund, and Meade (1972) have made similar comments on the positive side effects that have occurred from the operation of that evaluation system. To be sure, these are soft indicators, perhaps with the exception of the Guide-to-Goals effect. However, when combined with what we presume to be very strong prior belief in the efficacy of such procedures, there is probably enough reason to proceed with this self-evident agenda for human services improvement from the consumer's point of view.

References

Baxter, J., and Beaulieu, D. "Evaluation of the Adult Outpatient Program, Hennepin County Mental Health Service." In J. Baxter and D. Beaulieu (Eds.), *Program Evaluation Project Report, 1969-1973.* Minneapolis, Minn.: Hennepin County Health Service, 1974.

Calsyn, R., and LaFerriere, L. "Goal Attainment Scaling: An Effective Treatment Technique in Short-Term Therapy." *American Journal of Community Psychology,* in press.

Davis, H. "Change and Innovation." In S. Feldman (Ed.), *Administrators in Mental Health Services.* Springfield, Ill.: Thomas, 1973.

Drucker, P. *Managing for Results.* New York: Free Press, 1964.

Evaluation and Change, 4, 1977.

Fairweather, G., Sanders, D., and Tornatsky, L. *Creating Change in Mental Health Organizations.* New York: Pergamon Press, 1974.

Galano, J. "Treatment Effectiveness as a Function of Client Involvement in Goal Setting and Goal Planning." *Goal Attainment Review,* 1977, *3,* 17-32.

Houts, P., and Scott, R. "Goal Planning in Mental Health Rehabilitation." *Goal Attainment Review,* 1975-1976, *2,* 33-51.

Jones, S., and Garwick, G. "Guide to Goals Study: Goal Attainment Scaling as Therapy Adjunct?" *P.E.P. Newsletter,* 1973, *4,* 1-3.

Kiresuk, T., and Schultz, S. "Tailoring Evaluation to Measure the Accountability of Mental Health Services to Women." Paper presented at Evaluation Research Society Annual Meeting, Washington, D.C., 1978.

Kiresuk, T., and Sherman, R. "Goal Attainment Scaling: A General Method of Evaluating Comprehensive Community Mental Health Programs." *Community Mental Health Journal,* 1968, *4* (6), 443-453.

Kiresuk, T., and others. "Translating Theory into Practice: Change Research at the Program Evaluation Resource Center." *Evaluation,* 1977, *4,* 88-95.

Klerman, G. Address to the Psychotherapy Research Society, Toronto, Canada, 1978.

Lombillo, J., Kiresuk, T., and Sherman, R. "Evaluating a Community Mental Health Program—Contract Fulfillment Analysis." *Hospital and Community Psychiatry,* 1973, *24,* 760-768.

Roy, C., and Kiresuk, T. "Goal Attainment Scaling: Medical/Correctional Application." Paper presented at Sixth World Congress of Psychiatry, Honolulu, Hawaii, 1977.

Smith, D. "Goal Attainment Scaling as an Adjunct to Counseling." *Journal of Counseling Psychology,* 1976, *23* (1), 22-27.

Spano, R., Kiresuk, T., and Lund, S. "An Operational Model to Achieve Accountability for Social Work in Health Care." *Social Work in Health Care,* 1977, *3* (2), 123-142.

Spano, R., and Lund, S. "Management by Objectives in a Hospital Social Service Unit." *Social Work in Health Care,* 1976, *1* (3), 267-276.

Stelmachers, Z., Lund, S., and Meade, C. "Hennepin County Crisis Intervention Center: Evaluation of Its Effectiveness." *Evaluation,* 1972, *1,* 61-65.

Studer, S. "A Validity Study of a Measure of 'Readiness to Accept Program Evaluation.'" Unpublished doctoral dissertation, University of Minnesota, 1978.

Zusman, J., and Slawson, M. "Service Quality Profile: Development of a Technique for Measuring Quality of Mental Health Services." *Archives of General Psychiatry,* 1972, *27,* 692-698.

Thomas J. Kiresuk is chief clinical psychologist at Hennepin County Medical Center, Minneapolis. He teaches clinical psychology in the University of Minnesota graduate school and in the medical school's department of psychiatry.

Sander H. Lund is associate director of the Program Evaluation Resource Center and director of research for Evaluation and Change *magazine. He has written and consulted widely on topics related to program evaluation, planned change, and research utilization.*

Susan K. Schultz is a research associate of the Program Evaluation Resource Center and is also on the staff of Evaluation and Change *magazine. She has provided program evaluation consultation to a variety of agencies.*

The variety of contexts, the politics of each situation, and the availability of resources all dictate variations in assessing outcomes. Seven major principles of program evaluation are considered, along with a cautionary note to the ambitious who expect large program effects.

Outcomes, the Size of the Impacts, and Program Evaluation

Samuel Ball

It is an altogether reasonable proposition that we ought to assess the outcomes of the programs we evaluate. But it is an unfortunate fact that many things that are reasonable are not always a part of the practice of evaluative research. Frequently outcomes are not assessed in an evaluation. Rather, the program's *processes* are assessed and the assumption is made that if certain processes occur, then certain outcomes are bound to occur. For example, in a certain country, a nonformal education program is funded to help rural children accommodate to the needs of a more modern society — making them literate and providing them with certain work skills and attitudes. Yet the evaluation of this program concentrates on how many learning posts in how many

This chapter is adapted from the keynote address to the Anglophone West African Regional Educational Research Consortium on Educational Outcome Measurement and Design Considerations for Evaluative Research on Education, Monrovia, Liberia, March 27–April 6, 1978, and from selected chapters of Anderson, Ball, Murphy, and Associates, 1975.

villages were established, how many students were served by the program, and how well the staff in the villages communicated with the central staff. These are useful and important pieces of information of a *process* nature, but they cannot substitute for information on the final *outcomes* or *products* of the program. How well did the students learn? To what extent were attitudes changed? These are the crucial kinds of outcomes if we want to assess and interpret program attainments.

Outcome Assessment Principles

No single presentation can tell the world of program evaluation what to do in assessing outcomes. The variety of contexts, the politics of each situation, and the availability of resources all dictate variations. There is no single recipe; there is no formula to plug in as part of a mindless procedure. However, there are principles of program evaluation to consider, and there is the challenge and the stimulation involved in applying those principles to particular program evaluations. I consider seven major principles, stated as guidelines, and their applications in an educational evaluation setting.

First, *examine program goals. Are they being achieved?* This may seem self-evident. Of course, the evaluator will start in the quest for outcomes by looking at the program's goals and objectives. The problem is, however, that some programs are established with very vague goals, some with only process goals, and others without explicit goals at all. For example, a program on English as a second language may have as its major goal providing students with a comprehension of written and spoken English. This is a start, but it is vague. It does not specify for the evaluator (or, more important, for the program developers) the level of comprehension expected. Performance-level objectives are left to the imagination of the person examining the goals. Or consider the same program that states as its goals only the processes to be established. For example, all third- through fifth-grade students will receive four hours of instruction in English per week. As evaluators, we should be prepared to tell the educational policy makers whether this educational process occurred in the nation's schools. But with what results?

When the goals are vague, are not couched in terms of outcomes, or do not exist, it is up to the evaluator to have them made explicit. Two ideas come to mind. Talk to the program originators. Explain, in mild and politic ways, your problem as an evaluator and see if you cannot arrive at a set of explicit goals for the program, preferably worded in terms of the behaviors it is designed to foster in the recipients. After exposure to the program, what will students do that they cannot or do not currently do? And remind the reluctant program person that if the program is worthwhile, it should make a difference. "Let us look for that difference." A second idea (and a particularly valuable idea when the first one does not work) is to examine the program in detail as it operates and see what it is doing. How is it functioning? You as evaluator can infer what the program is trying to achieve by observing it in operation. The inferences can be discussed with the program directors and a consensus on intended program objectives can be reached on this provisional basis. Actually, this approach can be very provocative. It tells you the *function* of the program even if it does not tell you the goal.

Ideally, programs will be developed in the first place on the basis of program goals, and these goals, in turn, will serve as an excellent first step in specifying the outcomes to be assessed.

Next, *ensure that affective/motivational/attitudinal goals and behavioral outcomes are not being neglected in favor of cognitive/achievement goals as measured by paper-and-pencil tests.* It is relatively easy for the evaluator to turn to ready-made tests of educational achievement and aptitude when outcomes are being assessed. Is there a new reading program? Then find out how much improvement has occurred in reading. Use a reading vocabulary and a reading comprehension test that is available already. But is that sufficient? Does it cover the spirit of the program's goals statement (even if it covers the letter of the goals statement)? Is it not more important to find out whether the children *are* reading (when they have the opportunity) in contrast to whether they *can* read? Ninety-five to 98 percent of Americans can read. Less than 50 percent of them read a book last year. And would it be a useful procedure to assess whether the students enjoy their new reading lessons more than they did with the old program? Will students want to go on learning, or are they learning to hate school? The point is that the evaluator neglects to consider the affective and the behavioral outcomes of a program at the extreme risk of carrying out an evaluation that is incomplete and unsatisfactory.

Then, *use the "medical model" rather than the "engineering model" of evaluation.* Of the many ways to carry out evaluation studies of outcomes, the most typical involves a simple comparison of average gains for two groups, one of which has been exposed to the educational treatment or training program of interest. This approach has been called the engineering model of evaluation; it focuses upon input-output differences. It provides information necessary for assessing the *overall* significance or impact of a treatment or program, but this information is not sufficient for further development or revision of the program. If evaluative research is to provide a base of knowledge and understanding that will not only permit systematic program improvement but also justify generalizing the findings to other settings and problem areas and point to needed program modifications to cope with changing conditions, then the form it takes and the kinds of questions it asks must go beyond the typical engineering approach to a more complex research design. This more complex approach, which has been called the medical model of evaluation, goes beyond the engineering (input-output) approach in several ways.

The medical model recognizes that prescriptions for treatment and evaluation of their effectiveness should take into account not only the student's achievements but also other characteristics of the students and their ecology, context, or environment as well. This is essentially a call for a systems approach to program evaluation—that is, dealing with the interrelatedness of all the key factors (psychological, social, environmental, and educational) that may affect performance. Television, for example, not only increases knowledge; it also changes the way a person thinks and perceives and changes a person's social behavior.

Another obvious derivative of the medical model is a concern for monitoring possible side effects of the treatment. In addition to the intended outcomes of a program, we should also assess a wide range of possible outcomes, for in the process we may uncover some outcomes that ought to be considered in reaching a final appraisal of the program's value. A further implication is that feelings and reactions should be assessed periodically throughout the course of the treatment and not just at the beginning and at the end. As is the custom in exemplary medical practice, we should be concerned about attitudes toward the treatment itself.

Underlying the entire medical metaphor is the notion that whenever possible in evaluating educational programs, as in evaluating drugs, we should go beyond a simple assessment of the size of effects to an investigation of the processes that produce them. Only through an understanding of these processes will we be able to develop a rational basis for changing programs if conditions change and for identifying the types of potential side effects that should be monitored.

Thus, according to the medical model, educational research and evaluation should focus not only upon the outcomes of education but also upon the process and the context of education, thereby encompassing several broad areas of measurement concern—input, program, context, and outcome, and their relationships.

When we evaluated "Sesame Street" (Ball and Bogatz, 1970), a television series for preschool children, we first looked at the sixty or so series objectives. Next, we requested that some kind of priority be established; we then focused on assessing the twenty or so most important outcomes. But we did not stop there. We assessed the families and we did a content analysis of the program. And we asked other questions: Would the series cause children to view even more TV than they currently were viewing? Would mothers be likely to read less to their children (unintended negative side effects)? Would children who learn the names and sounds of the letters of the alphabet begin to learn to read words commonly found in the environment ("street" or "supermarket," for example)? And, looking at the long term, would children who viewed the show a great deal be more eager to learn about reading and arithmetic when they go to school (possible positive side effects)?

Of course, the evaluator has to be selective, but sticking to assessing intended outcomes can be as dangerous in education as it proved to be in medical research. (Recall the Thalidomide scandal, where a perfectly good tranquilizer [intended outcome] also maimed or killed thousands of embryos [unintended outcome].) Unfortunately for us, negative unintended outcomes in education are sometimes more difficult to detect than they are in drug evaluation. However, if we do not look for them, we are even less likely to find them.

Also, *consider whether to look for interactions between the program and different groupings of students.* An educational program is unlikely to have uniform effects upon all who are given it. Thus, I could argue that programmed instruction is more useful for anxious students and less useful for curious, spontaneous students. Open classrooms operate better for students who are used to having freedom and who can effectively regulate their own behavior. More structured classrooms are better for students who need direction from an authority figure. It is true, of course, that most studies of the interaction between the educational treatment and students' traits do not provide evidence of large effects. But it is reasonable to suppose that in some heterogeneous population groups, interactions between program treatment and kind of student could be considerable. In Indonesia, for example, what works effectively in social studies in Moslem Java is not as effective in Hindu Bali. In nations where the rural poor represent a group with quite different characteristics from the urban poor and where the same educational program is used for both groups, the sophisticated evaluator will look to see if outcomes vary on the rural-urban dimension.

The next step is to *consider long-term as well as short-term objectives.*

Recently, I was asked to review the design of an evaluation where all-day kindergarten classes were being contrasted with half-day kindergarten classes. The outcome measures all seemed reasonable but they also seemed incomplete. The evaluation study looked to see what children in the two treatments would be like at the end of the kindergarten year. But the evaluator should also have been concerned with what the children would be like at the beginning and the end of first grade.

Whenever the results of successive measurements are to be used to document change, the measurements should be as comparable as possible. The evaluator must attend to comparability both in the instruments and in the data collection schedule and procedures. For example, one vocabulary test may not be comparable to another (even two equated test forms may differ enough to upset a study of gains); measurements taken just before an important holiday may not be comparable to measurements taken during a more normal period; interviews in the home may not be comparable to interviews at the training facility. The problem of obtaining comparable measures over time is worse in studies of young children, where it may not be possible to use the same types of measures across age levels or where the same measures have different meanings at different age levels. In such cases, investigators frequently use measures at earlier ages that are considered predictors or precursors or measures used at later ages. For example, children might be given visual and auditory discrimination tests when they are seven. Some purists argue, however, that a true longitudinal evaluation cannot tolerate changes in instrumentation across successive measurements. One approach to this dilemma is to administer measures according to an overlapping pattern.

It is not always possible to assess long-term outcomes. The funds may not be available; decisions cannot wait long enough; the evaluator cannot afford the expenditure of time. At least, then, the evaluator should indicate that the outcomes reported *are* only short-term outcomes.

Do not be afraid to assess outcomes just because of measurement problems. Many an evaluation has failed to assess an important outcome because the evaluator could not find an already available, reliable measure. Perhaps a number of more indirect measures of that outcome could be used. Each may have its own source of bias; but if each somewhat faulty measure indicates the program is successful with respect to the construct being assessed, then valuable evidence has been provided to the decision maker by the evaluator. For example, as previously indicated, one unintended outcome to be measured in the "Sesame Street" evaluation was amount of TV viewed by the child. Consider the problems in assessing the amount of TV viewed by a child at home. An observer sitting in the child's home would be obtrusive and very reactive. That kind of expensive observational measure would not do. However, there were measures we could use, although they, too, had problems: (1) asking the parent at the end of the week how many hours the child had viewed (would bring in biases associated with the parent's memory and desire to give the "correct" answer to the interviewer); (2) asking the child in the morning what had been viewed the day before (involved problems of sampling, with the question of whether one day, now and then, was a sufficient sample of the child's general viewing); (3) finding out with a simple test how familiar the child is with various TV programs (does the child recognize the main character, for example). This measure suffers from the confounding of amount of viewing and the learning and perceptual abilities of the child being interviewed. Perhaps a child views a lot and has a bad memory for faces. No single measure is highly reliable or without bias. But if the evaluation showed that, whatever measure of the construct is used, the outcome remains about the same, then the evaluator can claim with some better degree of confidence what that outcome is.

Before leaving this principle (*do not be afraid of the measurement problem*), the evaluator might want to consider the use of the kinds of checklists suggested in Table 1 and in Table 2.

Frequently, evaluators forget there are more ways of measuring a student's readiness than by testing the student with a readiness test. There are more ways of measuring a student's attitude toward school than by giving the student a school-attitude questionnaire. The adept evaluator does not sidestep the measurement problem but rather faces it head on—and usually overcomes it.

Finally, *establish evaluation priorities on outcomes*. I have outlined here a plan for a comprehensive assessment of outcomes based on program goals, on guesses as to unintended side effects, on a systems approach in which outcomes are looked at in relation to the program and its context, on consideration of affective, motivational, attitudinal, and behavioral outcomes, and on the need to examine outcomes for subgroups undergoing this program. This is a formidable undertaking. With such a comprehensive approach, the evaluator next should decide what should be judiciously attempted. What will the traffic bear? What resources are available—evaluator time, computer, data collectors, data collection time, and so on? Most important, what are the needs of those who want to use the evaluation? What are the decisions to be made? What information *must* the evaluator provide?

Usually, at this point the evaluator must cut back on the evalua-

Table 1. Data Sources for Evaluation Efforts

Who or What *Object of Measurement*	Why *General Class of Variables Measured*		How *Likely Data Collection Method*[a]	From Whom *Source of Information*[b]
Students, trainees (adult)	I.	Input,	A, B, C, D, E,	1, 2, 4, 7, 8,
	V.	Outcome	F, G, H, J, L, M, N	9
Pupils (children)	I.	Input,	A, B, E, F, G,	1, 2, 4, 6, 7,
	V.	Outcome	H, K, L, M, N	8, 9
Teachers, instructors	II.	Program,	A, B, C, D, E,	1, 2, 3, 5, 6,
	V.	Outcome	F, G, H, K, L	8
Program administrators	II.	Program,	B, C, D, F, G,	1, 3, 4, 6, 7,
	III.	Context,	K, L	8
	V.	Outcome		
Parents of pupils	I.	Input,	B, C, D, F, G	1, 3, 4, 5, 8
	III.	Context,		
	V.	Outcome[c]		
Other directly concerned adults (potential employers, admissions officers, etc.)	III. V.	Context, Outcome	C, F, G	1, 5
Classroom or direct instructional climate	II.	Program	B, C, D, E, F, G, H, K, L	3, 4, 5, 6, 8
Institutional/ organizational climate	II. III.	Program, Context	C, D, F, G, H, K, L	3, 4, 5, 6, 7, 8
Societal climate	III.	Context	C, F, G, H, J, K, L	5, 6[c], 7, 8
Data collectors	IV.	Assessment	A, B, C, D, E, F, G, K, L, M, N	1, 2, 4, 5, 8
Data collection procedures	IV.	Assessment	B, C, D, E, F, G, H, K, L	4, 5, 8

[a] A—test; B—situational test; C—questionnaire; D—log; E—film, tape; F—interview; G—records; H—physical trace; J—social indicator; K—ratings; L—observation; M—clinical examination; N—physiological measure.

[b] 1—self; 2—peers; 3—students; 4—teachers; 5—administrators; 6—parents (where program is for young children); 7—other adults; 8—observer; 9—clinician.

[c] Some programs, such as the parent-child centers, involve the mother as part of the instructional program. In such cases, variable class II, Program, is relevant here.

Source: Anderson, Ball, Murphy, and Associates, 1975, p. 116.

tion plan, knowing at least that the decision on what to cut is an informed decision—informed in terms of the alternatives. What actually gets done is not now what first jumped into the evaluator's head but what finally was decided upon after all serious possibilities were considered. Remember, an evaluation is useless if no outcomes can be reported because the evaluator has been drowned in a sea of data.

Size of Outcome Effects

I have presented seven major principles to consider in developing a set of outcome variables to be assessed in an evaluation. Not the least of the principles was the final one—*ensure that the evaluation is "doable."* Do not be too ambitious and take on too many outcome measures.

The question of ambition in program evaluation arises again (and in relation to outcomes) when we consider the question of outcome size. I start with the premise that you have to pity the poor evaluator, who is beset from all sides, especially when the size of program impact is in question. On the one hand is the program developer, who is usually very creative or very entrepreneurial and strongly believes in the program. Perhaps the strong belief is born of crass hopes for commercial success; perhaps, and far harder to deal with, the program developer's strong belief is born of an overweening confidence in the virtue of personally developed ideas and plans. And there is no doubt that both kinds of educational program developers exist. They have in common a steadfast expectation that the evaluation should indicate the program has been remarkably effective—that it has produced "slam-bang" effects, a great innovation doing for education what Beethoven did for classical music (for the dedicated program person) and what Kentucky and Colonel Sanders did for chicken (for the crass commercialist).

At the other extreme is the hardheaded, research-oriented evaluation critic. This person, who may never have carried out an evaluation, has a burning mission that transcends carrying out evaluations, and that is to unmask any evaluation result that seems to suggest an educational program is working effectively.

"Was there a random sample of all children who could possibly be involved in the program? Aha! See? Limited generalizability!"

"Do you have the results of a five-year follow-up to show it is having a continuing positive impact? Not yet? Aha! Only a short-term impact has been shown!"

Table 2. Methods of Assessing Learning

Assessment Mode	Definition/Description	Illustration/Examples	Advantages — When Used	Problems	Considerations
Work Sample	Realistic representation of the task	In order to measure Jan's ability to hire new personnel as office staff, she conducts an interview with a prospective employee in a controlled setting	Especially appropriate in the case of competencies that focus on what one is able to do with knowledge rather than upon knowledge itself or products produced as a result of performance	How representative is it of the real situation; and how comprehensive	Be certain the test represents what happens in performance in a natural situation
	Requires the accomplishment of a specific task in a controlled setting	(Make into a school activity, e.g., chair a class meeting)	Used when difficult or expensive to measure in natural setting	Both necessary for valid results	Should be representative sample of actual performance on the job
	Attempts to reproduce important parts of the actual job		Evaluates ability to execute an action, process, or task	Bias possible on part of observer; observer might not be able to note all relevant behavior; therefore, good to have two or three observers	Should be judged by more than one expert to obtain good reliability

I. Performance Tests

Situational Observation (Unobtrusive)	The candidate is engaged in some realistic task	In order to measure Ted's salesmanship competency, two of his supervisors accompany him at various times as he is working with a potential customer	When other means are not available, appropriate for measuring application of knowledge, including employment and volunteer activities	High cost factor	Record behavior, categorize according to criteria predetermined, use rating scale or checklist, make judgment
Mode: Live/ Audiovisual	Assessor observes behavior in a natural setting	On-site visitation		High cost factor	
				At times, difficult to control variables	

Source: Adapted from Knapp and Sharon, 1975.
Note: The original piece provides a comprehensive listing. Table 2 is only a small sampling of that listing.

"Are the assessment techniques for the dependent variables based on the program's goals? They are? Tailor-made tests; but can you show the program has impact on *other* areas? Oh, I see—the program's impact has only limited range."

And on it goes. Even if the evaluator shows the program has been moderately effective, the ardent program people will still feel devastated and betrayed. Stuck with their uncritically high expectations (remember how Head Start would practically wipe out the educational effects of disadvantagement?), the news of moderate success is as appealing as finding out you were only three off winning the state lottery. By the same token, an evaluator with the same news of moderate success is likely to be taken strongly to task by the hardheaded researcher for "overdramatizing" the results—for not being critical and cautious enough. So I begin this section by pitying the poor evaluator.

Just what constitutes an important outcome in education is clearly a debatable issue. We know it is not a matter of checking a ratio, as, for example, in an F test. Statistical significance helps us decide if a difference is believable, but it does not tell us whether the difference is important. Nor is it good enough to use a rule of thumb such as "It improved scores by more than half a standard deviation." What are some of the considerations we should take into account when assessing the importance of the outcomes of educational programs? And why do relatively few educational programs seem to provide the big impacts we humanitarians would like to see provided? Why do we so rarely come up with massive and compelling results? Let us examine these intertwining questions (see Sechrest and Yeaton, this volume).

Educators as Narcissists. In education, we have the notion that formal educational programs are the major source of educational growth and development. We look into the pool of educational process and all we see is ourselves. We forget parents and families. We ignore peer groups. We oversimplify and we assume that if our educational treatment is effective, it will do wonders. For example, instead of forty children per teacher, we will try thirty. Or we will add a teacher aide to the classroom. Or we will adopt a new reading curriculum. But the students still have the same social and economic environment at home, the same friends, the same television or radio programs, the same attitudes toward the school, the same values and expectations, the same teachers—indeed, all we have changed in many educational programs is one or a few of the myriad causal agents affecting student performance, one link in a complicated webbing of causal chains. A given educational treatment is but one part of the student's total socialization package.

Incremental Effects. A closely related point is that even in terms of short-term outcomes in a given subject area, the particular innovation in a school curriculum is not the *alpha* and *omega* of the child's source of learning even in that curriculum area. When we assessed the impact of "Sesame Street," we found some rather large differences ascribable to preschool-aged children viewing the show. When we assessed the outcomes of "The Electric Company" (Ball and Bogatz, 1973), a television show to teach reading, we got no such large differences anywhere. We got statistically significant differences due to viewing (with thousands of subjects and hundreds of classrooms), but not a slam-bang outcome. Why the difference between "Sesame Street" and "The Electric Company"? For many of the children, "Sesame Street" was the only educational experience they received in such areas as letter and number recognition; "The Electric Company" was just a part of the reading curriculum. All children (viewers or not) were receiving reading instruction. Thus, "The Electric Company" provided only an increment to the learning already occurring.

To illustrate this point further, if you want a slam-bang outcome, take a group of eight-year-olds who are nonswimmers, teach half to swim using an intensive summer swimming program, and let the other kids play soccer. Then test them all in swimming. Or take a group of six-year-olds, let them live in Francophone Africa for six months, and then compare their oral French to a control group left back home in Anglophone Africa. You are certain to show a slam-bang outcome. But this is not like the educational treatments we usually evaluate.

The problem of the comparison group is a recurring one in interpreting effect size. We looked at the example of "Sesame Street" versus "The Electric Company," showing how the choice of a comparison group makes a huge difference in deciding whether we have a seemingly large effect or not. In the one case, the control (comparison) group had little experience in the content taught the treatment group. In the other case, both groups were receiving instruction in the content defined by the treatment. This is perhaps especially relevant to the evaluation of compensatory education programs. What is the level of expected performance against which we try to interpret the program's effectiveness? There is also a political problem embedded in this issue. Consider a group of disadvantaged children in a rural setting. Learning occurs, of course, but at a low rate; and perhaps it occurs among the older children at a decelerating rate compounded by high levels of absenteeism. Now consider further the installation of a new program in which the children learn at a rate still below the national norm, but much better than before. Is that a slam-bang outcome? If we say yes, we are in danger of arguing (or being accused of arguing) we have different and lower expectations for rural children, that we are in league with or sympathetic to intellectual viewpoints antithetical to the interests of these children, that we are happy or at least satisfied with inferior performance by those children. We must, therefore, point out in our reports that a big improvement has occurred and that there is room for even more improvement.

The Treatment. A program is not necessarily a single, unitary treatment. National programs may begin conceptually as one treatment, but they usually become many treatments, each mediated by states, local education authorities, school districts, schools, and teachers. Some of these treatments, I suspect, are not just slam-bang—they are double dynamite; but others are not. Overall, on the average, across all treatments we usually find moderate results. We could adopt a different evaluation stance—identify the excellent programs and the inept ones and describe what the good and bad treatments are like. We could then indicate which elements in the national programs seem to work well and which do not. However, policy makers do not usually want a description of the good and bad spots; they want to know the size of the overall outcome. And almost immediately, if the program is in fact many different treatments, we have to expect that some of those treatments will pull down the average.

Quality versus Quantity of Outcome. There is an important distinction to be made between the quality and the size or quantity of the outcome. Worthwhile effects in education involve important variables and large impacts. *Ersatz* effects in education involve trivial variables that just happen to be associated with impressively big impacts. We can tell whether an outcome is important and nontrivial by systematically surveying experts; and other relevant people's opinions. Maybe we can get a consensus. We can tell how big the outcome is if we use a measure tuned to the specific program, its content and its teaching approach, which provides tailor-made, domain-referenced assessments. We may get large-looking outcomes, but we are open to the criticism that these are contrived. If we try to measure more general kinds of educational effects (like improving aptitude for school learning), perhaps using some standardized tests, then we are likely to do an injustice to the size of the specific effect because our instruments are not sensitive to the epicenter of the programs' impacts—they assess instead the peripheral after-effects of the initial bang. For example, if we teach the child letter sounds, counting, and matching of a letter and number shapes and test impact by some standardized reading readiness test in which only a small part of the test reflects this curriculum, then we are doomed not to find a big impact. Or suppose we try to enhance the child's self-esteem with respect to schoolwork and administer the Coopersmith Self-Esteem Scale. That sounds like a nice match. But if we were to break the tradition and inspect the items on the scale, we would find that only a small percentage of them refers to academic self-esteem. The rest deal with such matters as how much other kids like me and how good-looking I am. Important outcomes should involve general achievements as well as specific learnings. But it is unfair to expect a given treatment, all on its own, to provide such an impact. A number of treatments, each providing specific effects, may lead to an overall general impact of appreciable size.

Conclusions

I have pointed out that conclusions about the size of outcomes are unlikely to meet with the approval of the program developer unless the evaluator can describe a really big impact. And if such an impact is claimed, there will be other critics who will question the evaluator's sanity or probity or both.

I have pointed out the difficulty of seeing big impacts because the educational process is so complex with so many causal agents operating that a modification in one agent is unlikely to have such a huge impact. However, you can make an outcome look impressive if you choose your comparisons wisely. Compare a program to no program and you see a big difference. Compare poor children's performance in a new program to how they might otherwise have performed—not to how rich children typically perform—and you are more likely to see a big improvement. You have a better chance of seeing big effects if you examine excellent examples of the treatment and if you restrain yourself from averaging the effects of a multitude of miscellaneous treatments fondly grouped under a specific title. And, as a final note for those in search of impressive outcomes, I advise testing for the specific elements taught in a program rather than for more general learnings achieved through some transfer-of-training process. Children learn best what we teach directly. If you want to guard against the charge that your tailored-to-the-curriculum tests assess the trivial, make sure you can document that the curriculum and the test indeed represent important skills and knowledge.

I doubt that we shall often uncover many huge and impressive outcomes in our program evaluations, but I also doubt that should concern us. Rather, I think we should be realistic and mark well the words of Gilbert, Light, and Mosteller (1975, pp. 39–40), who, having examined a large number of excellently designed positive evaluations, concluded, "[W]e find few with *marked* positive effects. Even innovations that turned out to be especially valuable often had small positive effects— gains of a few percent. . . . Because even small gains, accumulated over time, can sum to a considerable total, they may have valuable consequences for society. In addition, understanding the causes of even small specific gains may form a basis for evolutionary improvements in the programs." So if you don't find big impacts with your outcome measures, be realistic and do not despair.

The program evaluator, when called upon to assess the value of an educational program, has to handle a complex task in a complex setting. Nowhere is the complexity clearer than in the decisions that occur in choosing rationally what outcomes to assess. And the design of the evaluation is crucial to the interpretation of the importance and of the size of the outcomes. These are the topics addressed in this chapter. With the aid of the principles presented, with the application of good common sense (which is not so common), and with practice, the evaluator will be able to approach the problems involved with a true confidence. We cannot arrive at ultimate truth in program evaluation. But we are not floundering around, flaunting our feelings, guesses, and intuitions. We can provide useful information about educational programs. That is the challenge of our profession and we can and must meet that challenge.

References

Anderson, S. B., Ball, S., Murphy R. T., and Associates. *Encyclopedia of Educational Evaluation Concepts and Techniques for Evaluating Education and Training Programs.* San Francisco: Jossey-Bass, 1975.

Ball, S., and Bogatz, G. *The First Year of Sesame Street: An Evaluation.* Princeton, N.J.: Educational Testing Service, 1970.

Ball, S., and Bogatz, G. *Reading with Television: An Evaluation of the Electric Company.* Princeton, N.J.: Educational Testing Service, 1973.

Gilbert, J. P., Light, R. J., and Mosteller, F. "Assessing Social Innovations: An Empirical Base for Policy." In C. A. Bennett and A. A. Lumsdaine (Eds.), *Evaluation and Experiment.* New York: Academic Press, 1975.

Knapp, J., and Sharon, A. *A Compendium of Assessment Techniques.* Princeton, N.J.: Educational Testing Service, 1975.

Samuel Ball is professor and head, Department of Education, University of Sydney, Australia. He is also editor of the Journal of Educational Psychology. *He has coauthored books and articles on program evaluation with the series editor, Scarvia Anderson.*

Index

New Directions Quarterly Sourcebooks

New Directions for Program Evaluation is one of several distinct series of quarterly sourcebooks published by Jossey-Bass. The sourcebooks in each series are designed to serve both as *convenient compendiums* of the latest knowledge and practical experience on their topics and as *long-life reference tools.*

One-year, four-sourcebook subscriptions for each series cost $18 for individuals (when paid by personal check) and $30 for institutions, libraries, and agencies. Single copies of earlier sourcebooks are available at $6.95 each *prepaid* (or $7.95 each when *billed*).

A complete listing is given below of current and past sourcebooks in the *New Directions for Program Evaluation* series. The titles and editors-in-chief of the other series are also listed. To subscribe, or to receive further information, write: New Directions Subscriptions, Jossey-Bass Inc., Publishers, 433 California Street, San Francisco, California 94104.

New Directions for Program Evaluation
Scarvia B. Anderson, Editor-in-Chief

New Directions for Child Development
William Damon, Editor-in-Chief

New Directions for College Learning Assistance
Kurt V. Lauridsen, Editor-in-Chief

New Directions for Community Colleges
Arthur M. Cohen, Editor-in-Chief
Florence B. Brawer, Associate Editor